An Anthropological Toolkit

An Anthropological Toolkit

Sixty Useful Concepts

David Zeitlyn

berghahn
NEW YORK · OXFORD
www.berghahnbooks.com

First published in 2022 by
Berghahn Books
www.berghahnbooks.com

Library of Congress Cataloging-in-Publication Data

Names: Zeitlyn, David, author.
Title: An anthropological toolkit : sixty useful concepts / David Zeitlyn.
Description: New York : Berghahn Books, 2022. | Includes bibliographical
   references and index.
Identifiers: LCCN 2022019381 (print) | LCCN 2022019382 (ebook) |
   ISBN 9781800734708 (hardback) | ISBN 9781800735354 (paperback) |
   ISBN 9781800734715 (ebook)
Subjects: LCSH: Anthropology--Dictionaries.
Classification: LCC GN11 .Z45 2022 (print) | LCC GN11 (ebook) |
   DDC 301.03--dc23/eng/20220601
LC record available at https://lccn.loc.gov/2022019381
LC ebook record available at https://lccn.loc.gov/2022019382

British Library Cataloguing in Publication Data

A catalogue record for this book is available from the British Library

ISBN 978-1-80073-470-8 hardback
ISBN 978-1-80073-535-4 paperback
ISBN 978-1-80073-471-5 ebook

https://doi.org/10.3167/9781800734708

Contents

Figures

Acknowledgements

I am very grateful to Michael Carrithers and Michael Herzfeld, who made extremely helpful comments on early drafts of this book and who have encouraged me to think about the shape of the general argument as well as some of the details. Ben Taylor-Green and Roger Just read drafts and gave useful feedback. Anna Rayne suffered the early writing and forced me to say what I meant. If the writing is any good, this is her doing not mine. Argument may be a partnership, but beyond that I need to thank her *properly*.

Introduction

This book promotes an eclectic, multifaceted anthropology in which multiple approaches are applied in pursuit of the limited insights that each can afford. I present summary discussions of various theoretical terms applicable to many social sciences. These are given as an alphabetical list as a means of considering an eclectic set of theoretical ideas that are helpful for the social sciences. I do not endorse any one of these ideas as supplying an exclusive path to enlightenment: I absolutely do not advocate any single position. As a devout nonconformist, I hope that the following sections provide material, ammunition and succour to those undertaking nuanced anthropological analysis (and their kin in related disciplines). This is not a manifesto for yet another 'turn'.

Mixing up or combining different ideas and approaches can produce results that, in their breadth and richness, are productive for anthropology and other social sciences, reflecting the endless complexities of real life. This is my response to the death of grand theory. I see our task as learning how to deal with that bereavement and how to resist the siren lures of those promising synoptic overviews.

My proposition, as a self-consciously synoptic overview, is that:

all overviews are misleading and inadequate (and always will be)

and its corollary:

do not try to develop one.

Instead I think we should embrace an eclectic anthropology. This requires consideration of the task at hand followed by careful choice of the theories best suited to achieve that task. The ethnography, and the questions we ask about it, will inevitably be influenced by the theoretical stances adopted (as well as reciprocally influencing them). So it is productive to view the subject through a variety of different lenses, adopting one day a structuralist approach, the next day a Marxist one, another day a phenomenological, then perhaps a realist one, and finally trying out an ontological one. Such eclecticism accommodates and reflects what Nancy Cartwright calls a 'dappled world', which is described by rules that form 'a patchwork not a pyramid' (1999: 1). Invoking another metaphor, David Sutton, discussing Sahlins' theory of history as applied to cooking in Greece, makes the point that cookery can also be a useful metaphor for theory (2018: 99), so this book could be seen as a listing of the ingredients for an anthropological soup.

As a parenthesis, I am aware that placing so much emphasis on the ethnography takes me a long way from the free-for-all of old-style postmodernism. Although this book is about theory, at heart it is not theory-driven. The Coda presents a small incident I observed during fieldwork in Cameroon together with my reflections on it, as an example of what dappled ethnography might look like. It illustrates the sort of excursions on which ethnographic research can take us: meandering journeys, following where the data lead us, and sometimes involving unexpected and fruitful deviations (Just and Zeitlyn 2014). This approach contrasts starkly with the strictly predetermined routes of (now sometimes preregistered) hypothesis-driven data gathering.

My intention here is to explore a different sort of anthropology: one without a master- (or meta-) narrative. Imagining what anthropology would be like without a meta-narrative is a type of thought experiment. If we can remove the pin from the Gordian knot of Grand Theory, then we might conclude that we are better off without it. Such a move belongs to what Michael Herzfeld called the 'militant middle ground' (1997: 165 ff). Several articles in the journal *Anthropological Theory* endorse this sort of approach, one that Bruce Knauft describes as putting 'anthropology in the middle' (2006) along with Herzfeld's own reconsideration of anthropological realism (2018), which also belongs in this middle ground.

Looking back at a previously dominant theoretical figure, I am both for and against Lévi-Strauss. For him, I would say that bricolage is all there is; against him, that he assumes that a social group has a relatively simple underlying structure. I am for the randomness, the continually extemporised re-creation that makes and remakes society anew but in ways that are recognisably influenced by and dependent on what went before (there is an echo of Darwinian logic in this phrasing). This is a form of constraint, but it is not a determining pattern. There is no architect. There is no single 'structuring structure', as Anthony Giddens put it. (As a parenthetical note on Giddens, which is worth making here: if *many* structuring structures exist, then the resulting picture is very different from that which a *single* structuring structure would produce, especially if the many structures potentially conflict with one another. I would be very happy with an account that allows for multiple structuring structures.) My quarrel is with those who think they have identified the one true course, the single most important thing about human society. I believe that no such thing exists and that to assert its existence is at best misleading and at worst seriously misrepresents the worlds we live in.

These worlds are replete with emergent properties that mislead: generations of theorists have inferred underlying structures on the basis of emergent, hence second-order, properties. My claim is that these inferences are often unwarranted: no underlying structure is necessary to explain the emergent properties. In his re-examination of Marcel Griaule's oeuvre, Andrew Apter makes a similar point: 'In this case, Griaule is succumbing to the synoptic illusion (Bourdieu 1977: 97–109), when practical systems of classification are abstracted into a fixed hierarchy of logical relations apart from their context-specific validity, and thus appear contradictory' (Apter 2005: 118).

Understanding Social Worlds: Metaphors for the Task

My recent work on photography leads me to use a visual metaphor first. An aural one is considered below.

The approach I am advocating evokes the early cubism of Braque or Picasso, rather than the single viewpoint of photography or perspective-based landscape painting. Marcel Griaule exemplifies this issue. Having served in the First World War as an aerial photographer, he later worked with the Dogon in Mali and fantasised about the 'perfect view' that aerial photography could provide of a society (1937: 469–74). (Echoes of this fantasy are found in the discussions and controversies surrounding Google Earth and Google Streetmaps.) The aerial photograph exemplifies or concretises the panopticon (designed by Jeremy Bentham in 1785), which Foucault describes as the embodiment of power, part of the process by which the power of the state becomes incorporated into an individual's body. There is a chain of connection from this sort of optical tyranny to the colonisation of the eyes, and the claim that seeing is possessing (see Wolf 1990).[1] To return to the cubist parallel, the facets of a cubist painting show different aspects of the object portrayed, which may not be simultaneously visible in reality (such as the forehead and the back of the head) but which conventionally we infer: when we are shown a face, we suppose the skull behind it. By combining elements from mutually exclusive perspectives, cubist painters made us aware of our unceasing and unconscious attempts to fill in the invisible armatures that hold together the little we see at any one moment. Cubism forces us to acknowledge this process of filling in the gaps: the (usually tacit) assumptions we must make in order to make sense of the world. As researchers, we should be conscious of background assumptions about how social worlds are made. Such presumptions might mislead, so caution must be taken. As researchers, it is essential that we consciously scrutinise and verify our background premises lest they cause us to misconstrue events.

The second metaphor for understanding social worlds is aural. On my account, the sound of life does not have a single underlying, unifying theme or motif. Instead, the noise produced is closer to a cacophony, with many tunes played simultaneously in many different keys and registers. To consider noise is also to invoke its opposite: silence. This recalls Philip Peek's paper on sound (1994), in which he considers, among other things, how power is connected to silence: power can be manifested by restricting communication between office holders and others (such as kings and their subjects). Rulers cannot be addressed by their subjects directly, nor will they deign to address those subjects. Rather, in both cases rulers use a third-party mouthpiece. As a consequence, no one can speak back to them, further embedding the power imbalance. Jean-Pierre Warnier explored this theme in his analysis of Mankon manifestations of power in Cameroon (2007). Peek also considers masquerades and sound. In many places, it is not the mask's shape or costume that is important but the noise it makes. He suggests that a form of synaesthesia can be applied to aid an analysis:

> If we shift from our usual visual models and terminology to auditory models and terminology will we find the same conclusions from cultural systems? Rather than seeing what we can hear, what if we try hearing what we can see? It may be that the auditory manifestation is more essential and direct than the visual representation. (Peek 1994: 489)

By listening attentively, concentrating now on some frequencies and then on others, we can begin to distinguish elements in what at first sounded like an undifferentiated cacophony. With care, we can identify patterns and shapes in the sound, if not exactly tunes.[2] We may begin to hear how the noises of one year resemble (echo) but do not exactly reproduce those of previous years. Each performance (not only of ritual but also of many mundane social events) is a re-creation: even without a script, the performers remember what they did last time; they may try to do it again 'better' or just 'differently', perhaps making small changes because some performers and their instruments have been replaced by other performers using different instruments. A range of changes occur, from small incremental shifts to radical reinterpretations, as with classic tunes in jazz, each riffing on a theme. These processes are the motors of change (and also reflect change; both are possible).

I suggest that there are positive consequences of thinking about social worlds as cubist creations or repeated sound performances. Critically, if we adopt a multifaceted perspective, change becomes not just unsurprising but inevitable. This overcomes the problems of stasis that beset so many grand narrative theories (Marxism notwithstanding). The resulting analysis is always a fine balance: on the point of collapse but never quite, or never completely, falling down. The consequent lack of certainty (or dogmatism) is healthy and humbling. It makes us better anthropologists and possibly even better humans.

Theoretical Sparsity or Exuberance?

Sometimes I rail against theoretical exuberance, especially reliance on neologism. Some authors seem to see the coining of a new term as the answer to many and different problems, as if they were following the injunction 'if in doubt, then neologise' (or they invent a new meaning for an existing term). A curmudgeonly response to such exuberance would be to impose a near absolute limit on the number of permissible theoretical terms: whenever a new one is added, an old one should be jettisoned in its favour. But the purpose of this book is different: here I want to explore a wider range of concepts applicable to social sciences than are usually considered in theoretical discussions, in order to encourage theoretical breadth and productive eclecticism.

Notes for a Hypertext

Since I list the concepts in this book alphabetically, it should perhaps have only 26 sections, but since I prefer not to be a prisoner of formalism, some letters have more than one entry, others have none, and the length of the entries varies. In the end, I decided that although the organisational principle might be helpful it would be counterproductive to impose an artificial pattern on the sections, and so I have ended up with 60.

My selection of entries for inclusion inevitably involved decisions to omit. By and large, I have avoided discussing the larger and more heavily worn topics, such as functionalism, postmodernism, deconstruction and ontologies. One of my goals has been to explore the extent to which other theoretical positions are fruitful. So, for example, I include bifocality as an alternative to the ontological turn. More invidious choices had to be made between alternatives: which was the better head word, and which should merely be a cross-reference? Should there be one entry or two? For example, was it right to include an entry for *ironic detachment* with only a cross-reference to *bad faith*; to keep separate entries for *exemplars* and *vignettes* and for *essentially contested concepts* and *wicked problems*?

In planning this book, the question I asked myself was how to write about anthropological theory without making any specific theoretical argument. In other words, is it possible to practise anthropology without arguing for a single specific approach? My attempt to answer these questions has taken the form of a series of mini-essays about an eclectic collection of theoretical concepts that, over many years of anthropological practice, I have found helpful (or at least perplexing and tantalising, offering the promise of helpfulness or the prospect of thinking differently). In a similar spirit, Mieke Bal (2002) discusses some 'travelling concepts' and how they can be used to stay close to material being analysed while connecting to wider theory (since concepts are always connected to theories).[3] All such discussion is to encourage readers to consider what Peter Sohlberg and Håkon Leiulfsrud call the 'heuristic potential of homeless concepts' (2017: 8). The results add up, *indirectly*, to an argument for a dappled anthropology: one that not only accepts but revels in the muddled inconsistencies in people's conduct of their messy lives. However, for all the mess, there are discernible patterns in the way that people live their lives: the actors understand what is going on, they see an event unfolding in ways that are recognisable as belonging to a certain type. I suggest that if the actors can gain such understandings then so too can anthropologists and other researchers.

Patterns can become visible through forms of network analysis. By mapping the patterns of cross-reference in this book, we can see the interrelations of its *Hesse net* (see entry on this below). The full network diagram can be downloaded from the publisher's website.[4] It shows constellations of closely related terms and the importance of a few terms that link the different parts of the diagram. Two connecting terms that stand out are *finitism* and *ostension* (near the top right and bottom left of the diagram): neither of these terms features strongly in anthropological discourse. Another linking term, found at the top left, is *exemplar*, which has an interestingly uneasy relationship to the concept appearing near the centre of the diagram, *vignette* (which is why there are two entries and not just one). It may be that the distance between *exemplar* and *vignette* in the diagram is evidence of the difference between them: they have different sets of connections that distinguish the two concepts.

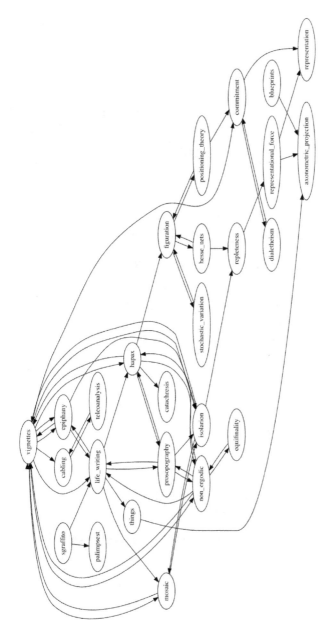

Figure 1. Central detail from the Hesse net or network diagram of cross-references between the concepts in this book. Image generated with Graphviz

Figure 1 shows an extract from the centre of the full diagram. The terms clustered in this detail are to do with dealing with the unrepeatability of everyday life and its representation. Although they may be similar to one another, individuals have their idiosyncrasies, and researchers have to make sense of these, seeing how the unique individuals they are dealing with nonetheless have resemblances to others in their group that can be *represented* in ways that are yet *faithful*.

Finally, the Coda, describing an incident recorded in my fieldwork and my reflections on it, is an illustration of tessellated or mosaic-ed ethnography. Of course this one fragment of ethnography cannot use or invoke all the ideas described in this book, but it is written with them in mind (and sometimes in conscious revolt against them). In terms of research, the two important tests are whether the analyst has gained a justifiable understanding of events observed and whether they have successfully conveyed that understanding to others.

A note on bibliography. In principle it would have been possible to write a book (or several) about each topic, and indeed many have been written. Attempting to make this text as readable as possible, I have tried to keep the bibliographic load to a minimum and give a separate bibliography for each entry.

Notes

1. This also connects to the 'erotics' of and the elements of epistemophilia in anthropology; that discussion must await another day.
2. Tina Campt encourages us to listen to the hum of archives in just the same way (2017).
3. As Neumann and Nünning (2012: 4–5) point out, precedents for this were made by Edward Said and James Clifford.
4. Also available from the Oxford Data Archive at https://doi.org/10.5287/bodleian:Kz2VqjXz6.

References

Apter, A. 2005. 'Griaule's Legacy: Rethinking "*la parole claire*" in Dogon Studies', *Cahiers d'Études Africaines* XLV (1) (177): 95–129.

Bal, M. 2002. *Travelling Concepts in the Humanities: A Rough Guide* (Green College Thematic Lecture Series). Toronto: University of Toronto Press.

Campt, T. 2017. *Listening to Images*. Durham, NC and London: Duke University Press.

Cartwright, N. 1999. *The Dappled World: A Study of the Boundaries of Science*. Cambridge: Cambridge University Press.

Griaule, M. 1937. 'L'Emploi de la Photographie Aérienne et la Recherche Scientifique', *L'Anthropologie* 47: 469–74.

Herzfeld, M. 1997. *Cultural Intimacy: Social Poetics in the Nation-State*. London: Routledge.

———. 2018. 'Anthropological Realism in a Scientistic Age', *Anthropological Theory* 18(1): 129–50.

Just, R., and D. Zeitlyn. 2014. *Excursions in Realist Anthropology: A Merological Approach*. Newcastle upon Tyne: Cambridge Scholars Publishing.

Knauft, B.M. 2006. 'Anthropology in the Middle', *Anthropological theory* 6(4): 407–30.

Neumann, B., and A. Nünning. 2012. 'Travelling Concepts as a Model for the Study of Culture', in B. Neumann and A. Nünning (eds), *Travelling Concepts for the Study of Culture*. Berlin: De Gruyter, pp. 1–22.

Peek, P.M. 1994. 'The Sounds of Silence: Cross-World Communication and the Auditory Arts in African Societies', *American Ethnologist* 21(4): 474–94.

Sohlberg, P., and H. Leiulfsrud. 2017. 'Conceptual Constructionism: An Introduction', in H. Leiulfsrud and P. Sohlberg (eds), *Concepts in Action: Conceptual Constructionism*. Leiden: Brill, pp. 1–22.

Sutton, D. 2018. 'Cooking in Theory: Risky Events in the Structure of the Conjuncture', *Anthropological Theory* 18(1): 81–105.

Warnier, J.-P. 2007. *The Pot-King: The Body and Technologies of Power* (African Social Studies Series, 17). Leiden: Brill.

Wolf, B. 1990. 'Confessions of a Closet Ekphrastic: Literature, Painting and Other Unnatural Relations', *Yale Journal of Criticism* 3: 181–203.

Sixty Words
to Think With

A Note on Cross-References

The sixty words considered here are listed alphabetically. Some entries end with cross-references to other directly relevant entries. These are marked 'Qv'. Less important cross-references (including heading numbers) appear in italics. The network diagram in the Introduction was constructed using both types of cross-reference. Some synonyms are included to direct readers to other entries e.g. *Astonishment: see Epiphany*.

A

Affordance; Agnosia; Aporia; Archaeology; Argumentation Theory; Autopoiesis; Axonometric Projection

1. *Affordance*

The notion of affordance nicely captures some of the complexity of human action, accommodating ideas of alternatives that are available but not chosen. We owe the idea of affordance (with its inverse of constraint) to Gibson, and it provides a nice alternative to determinism. A hammer enables (affords) the hitting of nails. So too does a screwdriver, although less efficiently: you can hold its shaft and hit the nail with the handle. The inverse is not the case: you cannot use a hammer to screw in a screw. So in the jargon we say that screwdrivers afford hammering, but hammers do not afford screwdriving. We should note that screws share some affordances with nails: a screw (but not a bolt) can be inserted with a hammer. So nails afford only nailing, while screws afford both screwing *and* nailing. There may be problems in establishing in the abstract what an object can or cannot afford, and the list of what it *cannot* afford is almost certainly infinite. This points to a problem with the idea: a hammer *can* do many different things, and *cannot* do even more. In order to produce 'sensible' lists of these cans and cannots, we need a set of background contexts that reveal the culturally appropriate stereotypical or exemplary usages. For European-style hammers, there is a contrast set between hammers and screwdrivers that points to inserting nails and not driving screws as being exemplars. But these cannot be straightforwardly inferred from the objects alone. (Does a hammer with a wooden handle have the affordance of keeping a fire going by serving as firewood? Yes, but only once. Tie a piece of string to a hammer or a screwdriver and it can serve either as a plumb bob or, after whirling, as a projectile weapon.) In the abstract, it is not straightforward to identify the contrast set for any specific object. (A similar set of issues concerns decisions to act or not to act: withholding or *forbearance*, §30.) In one sense there is a near infinite number of acts that I have chosen not to do, mainly by inadvertence, but often following from some previous action. That we cannot make a complete list of an object's affordances suggests that we should consider how useful the idea of affordance may be.

It is also unclear whether affordances must be consciously recognised. If not, then there are some parallels between affordances and functionalism that are concerning, since functionalism has fallen from favour while affordance has gained theoretical prominence. If some of a social institution's unintended consequences have the function of sustaining the status quo, then it may be appropriate to talk of that institution as having that affordance. This raises the question of whether affordances can be functions.

Such questions suggest that affordance may be an instance of a concept that promises too much: seeming to be clear and helpful but in fact rendered useless by potential infinite extension.

Another way of viewing the problem is to focus on constraints: what constrains an object's affordances? This seems to be a hard question to answer, bringing in a range of different culturally specific contextual information that determines how categories of objects can be used. To return to the example above, a hammer affords an enormous range of uses: as a doorstop, a murder weapon, a paperweight or even as large-scale printing type (as the letter 'T'). Perhaps we should talk rather of 'imagined affordances', where the prefix makes us consider the ensemble of person and object. The people doing the imagining will clearly have different cultural, physical and temporal specificities, so their imagined affordances of a single object may vary dramatically. The solution to both the potential infinite extension of possible affordances and the need for their cultural contextualising may be to invoke cultural salience. This allows for the acknowledgment that, of course, there is possibly infinite extension, but most of the time the list of possible affordances is kept small, manageable and shared. These are the most culturally appropriate affordances: the salient ones perhaps the first to be cited when people are asked to consider such things. This shows that social issues, politics and conceptual structures are all implicit in the consideration of affordances. If many people list similar affordances, this indicates that they share an understanding of what could be done with the object in question. However, what constitutes a shared affordance at one moment may be different at another time. So the affordances of smaller stones in 10,000 BCE (before the manufacture of glass) did not include smashing windows, and few people in Europe or North America would now list winnowing among the affordances of a tray. In unusual or changed circumstances, new affordances may emerge, and others may disappear. Far from being a fateful flaw in the concept, this demonstrates its useful flexibility.

Qv: *exaptation; finitism; forbearance*

References

Gibson, J.J. 1977. 'The Theory of Affordances', in R. Shaw and J. Bransford (eds), *Perceiving, Acting, and Knowing: Toward an Ecological Psychology*. Hillsdale, NJ: Lawrence Erlbaum, pp. 67–82.

Nagy, P., and G. Neff. 2015. 'Imagined Affordance: Reconstructing a Keyword for Communication Theory', *Social Media + Society* 1. DOI: 2056305115603385.

2. *Agnosia*

In medicine, agnosia is the inability to recognise things (persons, sounds, shapes or smells), usually following a brain injury. This becomes a theoretical model or metaphor for social science researchers not recognising what they are studying: being unable to comprehend what they have, in some sense, described. A classic example is describing parts of an elephant without considering the whole. Agnosia stands as a counter-example to claims that you need a concept to comprehend, a sample frame, a sortal system, or a description. Agnosia suggests that even with all these things we may still fundamentally misunderstand what is going on. Cases in point are how researchers from Europe or North America write about witchcraft in Africa, and how researchers from Africa explain the contemporary unimportance of religion in Europe. Hence agnosia suggests a salutatory caution. All description is theoretical in the sense that it needs a (theoretical) stance from which to start describing, and that that stance prescribes what the important features are and what should be omitted from the description: however, there is no guarantee that the resulting description is an accurate account of what is going on. We may suffer from agnosia without realising it. Later researchers with different interests may curse the incompleteness of their predecessors.

Discussing this issue, Judith Okely makes a distinction between *looking* and *seeing*, a distinction taken up more widely under the rubric of 'expert' or 'professional vision'. In Okely's example, it takes an experienced dairy farmer to *see* what an unskilled observer, who merely *looks*, would gloss over as 'just another cow'. In the entries for *ostension* and *exemplar*, I talk more about providing definitions by example: 'look, this is a stereotypical dog'. Agnosia sets some limits to this: I may be shown an exemplar of a dog, but can I see what I am being shown? A shared understanding or underlying cultural consensus is needed for ostension and definition by exemplar to succeed. Hence a connection to the emic/etic distinction: there could be an etic distinction with no corresponding emic one (in a linguistic example, termites and ants could both be referred to by one term). However, with effort, and possibly with difficulty, we can succeed in recognising agnosia. This is essential because guarding against it motivates not only our methods but the very reason for doing research.

Qv: *colligation; emic/etic; exemplar; ostension*

References

Goodwin, C. 1995. 'Seeing in Depth', *Social Studies in Science* 25: 237–74.

Grasseni, C. 2007. 'Communities of Practice and Forms of Life: Towards a Rehabilitation of Vision?', in M. Harris (ed.), *Ways of Knowing: Anthropological Approaches to Crafting Experience and Knowledge*. Oxford: Berghahn, pp. 203–21.

Okely, J. 2001. 'Visualism and Landscape: Looking and Seeing in Normandy', *Ethnos* 66: 99–120.

3. *Aporia*

An aporia is an impasse, an insoluble conundrum. A classic example was Buridan's Ass: equally hungry and thirsty and cruelly positioned halfway between food and water, hypothetically doomed to die because of its inability to decide whether first to eat or drink. An aporia is an impossible decision, with equally good reasons pulling in opposing directions. Some see these as contradictions, with conflicting poles or positions between which we are asked to choose. Examples include choices between universalism and relativism, is and ought, particular and universal, doubt and certainty (Stade 2018: 129–30). Decision-making can be fraught and even paralysing. When weighing up the available alternatives, some people employ more or less arcane technologies, including divination, to help them choose. Others just shrug their shoulders and get on with it, knowing that they could have jumped the other way. Aporias may be an artefact of intellectualism: the assumption that decisions are made for explicable reasons makes the inability to give reasons into a problem: this is labelled an aporia. However, this intellectual approach may not be a reliable or fair characterisation of how decisions are actually made, even those that are carefully considered. The historian Ged Martin provides some excellent examples of how hard it is to pin down what led to a particular decision being made (the process of decision-making), particularly when it is retrospectively recast *after the fact* as having taken place according to a hard rationalist logic. He cites the telling example of Edith Lyttleton, who spent time in 1900 debating whether to follow her husband to South Africa or whether to stay in the UK with her two-month-old baby. Despite finding many good reasons to stay, she awoke one morning to find that she had decided to leave (2004: 87).

Qv: *argumentation theory; incommensurability; wicked problems*

References

Martin, G. 2004. *Past Futures: The Impossible Necessity of History*. Toronto: University of Toronto Press.
Stade, R. 2018. 'Who Are We to Judge? Two Metalogues on Morality', in N. Rapport and H. Wardle (eds), *An Anthropology of the Enlightenment: Moral Social Relations Then and Today*. London: Bloomsbury Academic, pp. 119–32.

4. Archaeology

Archaeology meant something very different to Collingwood than it did to Foucault. As well as being a philosopher, Collingwood was a field archaeologist engaged in excavating and interpreting material evidence to try and create a historical narrative.

For Foucault, archaeology was more of a metaphor: a way of talking about the silent and invisible armatures that shape how a society thinks about itself. Collingwood thought of archaeology and history as fundamentally the same disciplines. Philosophically, he saw them as presenting a single set of interpretive problems requiring a similar critical attitude to data (1946: 491). He viewed the data as being essentially distanced from the present of the historian and the archaeologist. (Foucault made no such assumptions.) Crucially, Collingwood's archaeology places great emphasis on the questions that archaeologists (and historians) ask of the data. Because the questions change, each generation finds a new archaeology and history in 'the same' place or from 'the same' documents. People in every society look to the past, even if only to reject it in order to remake the world anew. So in a sense, all societies follow Collingwood as they produce and reproduce social structures – ways of living and being in the world.

References

Collingwood, R.G. 1946. *The Idea of History*. Oxford: Clarendon Press.
Foucault, M. 1972. *The Archaeology of Knowledge*. London: Tavistock.

5. Argumentation Theory

Argumentation theory is a formalism for representing arguments. More than that, it provides a way of moving beyond classical logic to provide a means to characterise informal logic, modelling the way in which people actually construct arguments. This ability to represent arguments as they occur in ordinary life enables the identification of different *styles* of argument (argumentation schemes). It allows us to consider the possibility that there are different *types* of argument, each of which may use different reasoning styles, rather than assuming that there is a single universal form of reasoning and argument. Mapping an argument obliges the researcher to try to understand what is being said, what is being invoked and, just as importantly, what is *not* being said. For anthropologists, the greatest interest may lie in the implicit assumptions: things so basic that they need never to be stated locally but that need to be spelled out explicitly for an anthropologist from a different tradition. Rhetoric theory has a technical word for this: *enthymemes* are missing or implicit premises that must be made explicit in order to map out the logic of an argument. The type of argument mapping associated with argumentation theory resembles the identification and tracing of the network of *commitments* (§16) entailed by utterances. The Argument Interchange Format (AIF) was developed to aid this task so that a researcher documenting (mapping) an argument avoids becoming the prisoner of a particular piece of software.

Argumentation theory is particularly associated with Douglas Walton (who died while this was being written, early in 2020). As I have suggested, argumentation theory provides researchers with a framework upon which to build accounts of how actual arguments unfold in everyday life. It can be used to discuss concepts as *positioning theory* (§47) does for people. Both rely on forms of *colligation* (§15) and *figuration* (§28) to identify the elements or positions in flux: here, what is being argued over.

Qv: *aporia*; *commitment*; *positioning theory*

Reference

Walton, D. 2009. 'Argumentation Theory: A Very Short Introduction', in I. Rahwan and G. Simari (eds), *Argumentation in Artificial Intelligence*. Berlin: Springer, pp. 1–24.

Astonishment: see *Epiphany*

Autobiography: see *Life Writing*

6. Autopoiesis

'What is life?' Humberto Maturana and Francisco Varela coined the term *autopoiesis* to describe a way of thinking about biological systems, and as an approach to answering the old question about what makes a living being alive. They and Luhmann have developed the idea with reference to social systems, such as human societies. The key features are self-consciousness and feedback loops, which enable self-consciousness to affect the subject in a self-reproducing system. The observer knowingly observes, knowing that observation makes a difference. This differs from the model of experiments in physics, one of the goals of which is to remove any impact of the apparatus. In autopoetic systems, participation and observation inevitably produce their own effects. Given the impossibility of removing them altogether, we should try to reduce them and, more importantly, seek to understand what they are and take them into account when discussing the system. This may sound prosaic, but it is actually an important factor in doing and writing up ethnographic research. The role of the anthropologist cannot be ignored and should not be written out of the final report. To some extent, it is better to see the anthropologist as 'the apparatus' of anthropology. We learn by getting things wrong (and sometimes by inadvertently upsetting people). The best response is to try to identify what our inadvertence revealed, in order to avoid repeating the mistake and so we can take note: making explicit records of what is often implicit and unspoken. Mistakes can be as simple as using the left hand to give or receive money, offering money when being given a gift, or failing to offer money when circumstances call for it. In order to distinguish between the last two instances, Gilbert Ryle's 'thick description' is needed to identify the difference (in his example) between a wink of the eye and a blink of the eye.

Tim Jenkins, discussing ethnographic fieldwork and the perception of everyday life, captures this nicely: 'The experience of anomaly is the basis that allows us both to escape from an impossible objectivity that eliminates the observer, and from a self-regarding subjectivity. Fieldwork is, once again, only a special case of a general condition' (1994: 445). He continues: 'Fieldwork is an adequate method of gaining social knowledge because it reproduces in all vital aspects the processes it is studying, the play of self-presentation and self-knowledge (to adopt Herzfeld's terms) in the creation of everyday life' (1994: 451).

References

Jenkins, T. 1994. 'Fieldwork and the Perception of Everyday Life', *Man* 29: 433–55.
Luhmann, N. 2008. 'The Autopoiesis of Social Systems', *Journal of Sociocybernetics* 6: 84–95.
Maturana, H.R. 1978. 'Biology of Language: The Epistemology of Reality', in G.A. Miller and E. Lenneberg (eds), *Psychology and Biology of Language and Thought: Essays in Honor of Eric Lenneberg*. London: Academic Press, pp. 27–63.
Ryle, G. 1971. 'The Thinking of Thoughts: What Is "Le Penseur" Doing?', In *Collected Papers. Volume 2*. London: Hutchinson, pp. 480–96.

7. *Axonometric Projection*

A drawing using axonometric projection contrasts with one using perspective projection. In the perspective drawing, parallel lines recede into the distance and meet at the horizon (the vanishing point). Contrastingly, in axonometric drawings, parallel lines stay parallel. The vanishing point is set at infinity, so lines recede in parallel. For engineers, the advantage of axonometric (also known as isometric) projection is that measurements on the drawing are the same in all three dimensions. However, the price of this is ambiguity in the overall drawing.

Yves-Alain Bois, in his essay *The Metamorphosis of Axonometry*, describes the uncanny liberation of the eye produced by this projection. In the axonometric 'there is no negation of depth; instead it is geometrically rendered "infinite": the eye is no longer fixed in a specific place, and the view is no longer trained and "petrified"' (Waghorn 2005: 100 quoting Bois 1981: 46).

Axonometric projection reminds us that classical perspective drawing is not the only way to represent space: alternatives exist. As with space, so too for conceptual matters: there are more ways than one to think about social phenomena. For Bois, 'Since axonometric projection abolishes the fixed viewpoint of the spectator and creates several possible readings of one and the same image, there are several different "ideologies" of axonometry' (1981: 42). Some readers might draw a parallel between this and the perspectivism of Viveiros de Castro. I am unsure whether that is a parallel or a perpendicular.

This topic connects with theory in general in that just as there is no view from nowhere (or from nowhen) so also there is no naïve or untheoretical approach to the world and how we understand it. However, the idea of *projections* (emphatically in the plural) can help us think about the ways in which we view the world (starting from any one viewpoint). Given an arbitrary starting point, there is more than one way of seeing (understanding) the world from it, more than one way of 'projecting' what we see. Part of the point of academic anthropology is the aspiration to neutrality, to a projection that is as even-handed as we can achieve granted our inevitable and recognisable biases. Holbein's famous anamorphic painting, *The Ambassadors*, illustrates the impossibility of adopting two viewpoints simultaneously: the viewer focuses either on the people (when a smear appears in the foreground) or on the skull (when some distorted people appear in the background). This is a practical demonstration of *incommensurability* (§33) and how to deal with it: the viewer can alternate between projections and come to appreciate both.

To emphasise the way that the projections used in drawing connect to social science representations, I conclude this section with a quotation by Peter Metcalf, reflecting on his long ethnographic involvement with people from inland Borneo. Metcalf discusses the conventionality of perspective drawing and the importance of the audience, the viewers, working with the same conventions as the artist. He says:

> In more familiar contexts ... the graphic effects of perspective are utilitarian and offer no such *frisson* [of disorientation]. An architectural draughtsman does not expect his drawings to be seen as anything other than sheets of paper on a table; the trick is for him to show first one view and then another, so allowing those familiar with their conventions to form a mental image of a structure. The power of the technique is vastly increased by computer applications that permit the generation of an unlimited number of views, but its conventions remain the same.
>
> The anthropological analogue of a draughtman's perspective is what we have come to call a 'situated' discourse – one providing a perspective – and it has been attributed similar virtues. Stuart Hall, for instance, argues that any monolithic conception of 'black' identity is subverted by taking account of the way that the work of Afro-Caribbean writers and film makers is socially and historically 'positioned'. Although ethnic histories have their own reality and are 'not mere tricks of the imagination', they tend to fix identities in a 'straight, unbroken line, from some fixed origin' (1996: 113). In contrast, he emphasizes a dialogic process, creating difference as well as similarity. What he wants is a multiplicity of views. (Metcalf 2002: 106–7)

Qv: *partiality*

References

Bois, Y.-A. 1981. 'Metamorphosis of Axonometry', *Daidalos* 1: 41–58.

Latour, B. 1987. 'Opening One Eye While Closing the Other … A Note on Some Religious Paintings', *The Sociological Review* 35: 15–38.

Metcalf, P. 2002. *They Lie, We Lie: Getting on with Anthropology.* London: Routledge.

Waghorn, K. 2005. 'AFK – Away from Keyboard, Place in The Sims Online', *"Inside Out", IDEA journal* 6(1): 97–106. Retrieved 1 July 2009 from https://doi.org/10.37113/ideaj.vi0.200.

B

Bifocal Ethnography; Blueprints, Scores and Maps; Boundary Objects

Bad Faith: see *Ironic Detachment*

8. Bifocal Ethnography

This is Nurit Bird-David's (2008) term for the way in which anthropology employs both a close and a distant focus. We do this either simultaneously or by repeatedly juxtaposing the two standpoints. On her account, we juggle our gaze between the different parts of bifocal lenses. Bifocality allows us to look closely in order to produce detailed case studies, and to adopt a wider horizon when using these case studies to question the analytic language used, so questioning the terms of analysis in the widest sense. This may have profound theoretical implications and importance. Indeed, this is one of the ambitions of the ontological turn (Holbraad and Pedersen 2017), which is not otherwise discussed here; perhaps they should more modestly have called it a bifocal turn and acknowledged Bird-David as well as Viveiros de Castro.

There is a strange particularity to the metaphor: spectacles, whether or not bifocal, have *affordances* (§1) that contact lenses do not. Wearers of glasses can push them down their nose and look over the top of the lenses, or squint around the edges to compare the uncorrected vision. This means that they can achieve some effects of multifocality that contact lens wearers cannot. But I am in danger of taking the metaphor too literally. Bifocal ethnography is a form of *controlled equivocation* (§23). It is a way of encouraging comparison and enabling generalisation through jumps, rather than by moving along a continuum. In film, jumping between viewpoints is achieved by *montage* (§14), while viewers of paintings such as Holbein's *The Ambassadors* must physically change their standpoint in order to jump between *projections* (§7).

In the terms of Ingold's more recent, controversial and polemical distinction, Bird-David's claim is that while doing ethnography we cannot help but do anthropology. What Ingold sees as a problem (since he treats ethnography as bad and anthropology as good, although a later version is more nuanced), I see as a positive boon. Bird-David points at the way that theory and case studies (in Ingold's terms: anthropology and ethnography) are mutually constitutive. They may even be represented as an ouroboros (the snake swallowing its own tail). Other metaphors that have been used to approach this idea are bootstrapping (pulling oneself up by one's bootstraps) and Neurath's boat (the repairing of a wooden boat at sea, one plank at a time). These notions point to the impossibility of starting with a clean slate. Everyone has their own idiosyncratic, culture-laden starting point (they are *partial*, §45), and every academic has to deal with this as they do their research. (Of course, outside academe there is huge variation in how self-conscious or reflective people are.) Theory gives us terms and concepts to help us understand our experiences, but sometimes we change the theories in the light of our experience. There is no point in asking which came first or which is more important: each needs the other. At the risk of repetition: without a framework we cannot make sense of what is going on, while events and how we make sense of them may well cause us to change our frameworks. Bifocality emphasises the mutuality between different viewpoints, even between *incommensurable* (§33) ones.

Qv: *equivocation; collage*

References

Bird-David, N. 2008. 'Feeding Nayaka Children and English Readers: A Bifocal Ethnography of Parental Feeding in "The Giving Environment"', *Anthropological Quarterly* 81(3): 523–50.

Holbraad, M., and M.A. Pedersen. 2017. *The Ontological Turn: An Anthropological Exposition*. Cambridge: Cambridge University Press.

Ingold, T. 2008. 'Anthropology is not Ethnography', *Proceedings of the British Academy* 154: 69–92.

———. 2017. 'Anthropology Contra Ethnography', *HAU: Journal of Ethnographic Theory* 7: 21–26.

9. Blueprints, Scores and Maps

Nelson Goodman discusses musical scores and the problems involved in thinking of them of as representations of music. Although they are 'musical representations', they are fundamentally different from sound recordings. A score is an instruction set, a how-to manual, enabling a musician (or a group of musicians) to re-create a piece of music. To call this a representation is to misunderstand the undertaking at issue. Goodman suggests 'notation' as an alternative term to representation: notation is part of a score, guiding the musicians as they produce and nuance their performances. Similarly, car repair manuals and blueprints are designed and intended for specific purposes, and those purposes have far wider implications than are usually thought of. The same is true of maps. Yes a 'map is not territory', but contrast the maps produced for atlases, for sailors and for airline pilots: the information provided is driven by the needs of potential users. Harry Beck's London Tube map is a case in point: it works excellently for route planning but is famously not a good topographical representation of places above ground. A related contrast can be found in a different topic: how to think about the future. This shows us that predictions differ from political manifestos. Sometimes (paraphrasing both Peter Drucker and Antoine de Saint Exupéry) the point is not to foresee the future but to make it. Acting changes the world even if that action is an attempt that fails. Teleology is important for understanding how humans act: they have goals and strive to achieve them, sometimes using blueprints or scores along the way.

As Anthony Vidler puts it, architects' drawings *produce* buildings, but they are not representations of them. In his words:

> the intersection of diagram and materiality impelled by digitalization upsets the semiotic distinctions drawn by Charles Sanders Peirce as the diagram becomes less and less an icon and more and more a blueprint – or, alternatively, the icon increasingly takes on the characteristics of an object in the world. ... An aesthetics of data, of mapped information, would in these terms differentiate itself from the diagrammatic functionalism of the modern movement as well as from the long-lived neo-Kantianism that has served modernism's aesthetic judgments since the Enlightenment. Modernism in these terms has shifted from a diagram that is rendered as an abstraction of an abstraction to one that is a diagram of a diagram. (Vidler 2000: 40–41)

Similar arguments were made by Goodman concerning musical scores: these are not representations of pieces of music but guides to their creation. Sometimes they are used in surprising ways when the circumstances originally presumed do not apply. If the instruments for which the composer wrote are not available, it is still possible to perform the music: even without an organ, a Bach fugue can be played on another instrument. Such adaptations are commonly called arrangements, and the arranger is usually credited. Perhaps this is a fitting model for the results of social science research: they enable the *performance* of understandings of social phenomena, not in the ways originally undertaken but nonetheless recognisably related. And successful research provides for an arrangement of understanding.

Qv: *axonometric projection*

References

Goodman, N. 1976. *Languages of Art: An Approach to a Theory of Symbols*. Indianapolis: Hackett publishing.
Vidler, A. 2000. 'Diagrams of Diagrams: Architectural Abstraction and Modern Representation', *Representations* 72: 25–43.

Bootstrapping: see *Bifocal Ethnography*

10. Boundary Objects

The idea of boundary objects was originally developed by Susan Leigh Star in a discussion of what constituted 'distributed artificial intelligence', challenging the significance of the Turing Test. On her account, 'boundary objects are those objects that are plastic enough to be adaptable across multiple viewpoints, yet maintain continuity of identity' (Star 1989: 37). Another excellent definition of a boundary object is 'an entity shared by several different communities but viewed or used differently by each of them'. (Strangely the quote is attributed to Star, but I have been unable to trace it.) She then found the idea helpful in a very different context when working on the history of the development of a natural history museum. Boundary objects link different groups of actors who are engaged in common or interconnected tasks. They may be used by different groups in different ways: Star contrasts the radically different uses to which 'the same' map may be put. The utility of boundary objects is that often their usefulness follows from their *not* being at the forefront of attention. Boundary objects are part of the infrastructure, taken for granted and invisible: we see through them rather than focusing on them, at least when they are working well. Only when they go wrong, or when a pesky researcher comes along asking odd questions ('wrong' questions) does the weirdness of these objects become apparent. Like *essentially contested concepts* (§24), boundary objects enable people to live complicated lives, to accomplish complex tasks together without necessarily sharing common goals (or perhaps beliefs). Seen in this way, boundary objects are devices for managing heterogeneity: a group may be constituted in various different ways, and it is not safe to assume that all its members share any particular characteristics. In other words, boundary objects are devices that people use (usually without the label) to manage heterogeneity, as well as devices that academic researchers invoke when giving accounts of how heterogeneous groups work together. Bruno Latour discusses much the same thing when he talks about 'immutable mobiles', although he is thinking about 'invariant' objects moving between different groups. Dan Sperber's idea of 'semi-propositional representations' is similar: the very lack of intentional commitment, and the vagueness that surrounds certain utterances, enables them to connect people who do not fully agree on meaning. All these authors are discussing ways of dealing with heterogeneity through shared things/terms that may not all be understood or thought about in the same way.

Star and Griesemer's article (1989) about the Museum of Vertebrate Zoology provides an example. Amateurs and professionals each with very different interests and understandings of the museum met in managing the provision and treatment of vertebrate skeletons, so these were the boundary objects in that case. A very different example is the role of divinatory techniques when clients consult a diviner. Their understandings of and involvement in the event may be radically different, but they meet over the discussion of the patterns being interpreted (Zeitlyn 2021). In Cameroon the spiders in their divination pots (or elsewhere, Tarot cards etc.) function as boundary objects.

There is now a large body of work, from social studies of science and many other disciplines, showing how boundary objects are used in a wide range of areas. Not only can they *mean* different things to different people but can be *used* differently by different people to accomplish different ends. They are perhaps the positive reflex to '*wicked problems*' (§60): they show how irresolvable dilemmas, instead of being resolved, can be 'made liveable with'.

Qv: *essentially contested concepts*; *exemplars*; *wicked problems*; *translation*

References

Latour, B. 1987. *Science in Action: How to Follow Scientists and Engineers Through Society*. Cambridge, MA: Harvard University Press.

Sperber, D. 1982. 'Apparently Irrational Beliefs', in M. Hollis and S. Lukes (eds), *Rationality and Relativism*. Oxford: Blackwell, pp. 149–80.

Star, S.L. 1989. 'The Structure of Ill-Structured Solutions: Boundary Objects and Heterogeneous Distributed Problem Solving', in L. Gasser and M.N. Huhns (eds), *Distributed Artificial Intelligence*. San Francisco: Morgan Kaufmann, pp. 37–54.

Star, S.L., and J.R. Griesemer. 1989. 'Institutional Ecology, "Translations" and Boundary Objects: Amateurs and Professionals in Berkeley's Museum of Vertebrate Zoology, 1907–39'. *Social Studies of Science* 19: 387–420.

Zeitlyn, D. 2021. 'Divination and Ontologies: A Reflection', *Social Analysis* 65(2): 139–60.

C

Cabling; Catachresis; Chronotopes and Chronotypes; Collage/Montage; Colligation; Commitment

11. Cabling

While landlubbers may talk loosely of *ropes*, sailors talk of *cables*. That quibble aside, the important contrast is between a cable and a chain, the latter being made by interlocking component pieces (links) so that the whole chain is only as strong as its weakest link. By contrast, a cable is a plaited set of fibres, each relatively weak, with no single fibre running its entire length. The strength of a cable is determined not by the strength of its constituent fibres but by its diameter: the thicker the cable, the larger number of fibres it contains and the stronger it is. Cables (or ropes) have been used in suggestive metaphors for academic argument in subjects including anthropology and archaeology. An overall argument is likened to a cable: it is based on a wide range of constituents, none of which is conclusive. But plait them together so that each benefits from the support of its neighbours and the result is a persuasive case, a generalisation of the idea of triangulation. The point of the metaphor is that we should aspire to make arguments that are like cables rather than chains, lacking any potentially fatal weak point.

Qv: *teleoanalysis*; *Hesse nets*

Reference

Wylie, A. 1989. 'Archaeological Cables and Tacking: The Implications of Practice for Bernstein's "Options Beyond Objectivism and Relativism"', *Philosophy of the Social Sciences* 19: 1–18.

Case Studies: see *Vignettes*; *Exemplars*

12. Catachresis

In rhetoric studies, catachresis describes the metaphoric extension of a term to cover things beyond the term's 'usual' range of
meaning. It is also used for forced or contradictory uses (e.g.
in poetry). This is useful in anthropology, where we are forever
doing violence to conventional meanings as we translate across
borders and between cultural and linguistic schemas. In so doing, we change or at least challenge the target languages (the
controversial status of Margaret Mead in post-WW2 USA may
be a case in point: her account of relatively untroubled adoles-
cence in Samoa served as catachresis to what growing up was
taken to be). In a connected usage, Miller discusses Henry James'
story 'The Figure in the Carpet' and calls a catachresis 'the odd
man out' (1980: 111). He talks about how metaphoric extension
or symbolic violence produces exceptionalism. I had previously
thought of 'oddity' (the oddity of anthropologists) in the sense of
otherness, but in this light it can be seen as 'matter out of place'
in Mary Douglas's wonderful phrase. This view has bite, since
anthropologists stereotypically travel to another place where
they 'stand out' as being foreign. Another way of describing the
anthropological project in general is to consider what one must
learn in order not to 'stand out' in this way. By making this learning explicit, we may end up 'stating the bloody obvious', but we
can also make powerfully explicit the tacit understandings that
are not usually voiced. There is another relevant aspect of the
idea of the 'odd one out': not only are anthropologists odd, but
we often find that our best informants are 'odd ones out' locally.
They might be viewed as odd because they are intellectuals, or
possessed of spirits, or because of other unusual attributes. We
flock together perhaps because of a shared sense of not quite
fitting in; we gather in ways not thought of by rhetoricians.

In the Monty Python film 'The Life of Brian' (1979), Brian exhorts the crowd not to follow leaders. They chorus his words back to him. He responds: 'you are all individuals'; the crowd replies in unison 'YES, WE ARE ALL INDIVIDUALS'. But then a single voice (Eric Idle's) says: 'I'm not'. It's a great comic line: the only person individual enough not to toe the line does so by denying his individuality. In Miller's terms, this is a cata-chresis, and that speaker is the odd one out, the very person an anthropologist would want to talk to.

Qv: *hapax*

Reference

Miller, J.H. 1980. 'The Figure in the Carpet', *Poetics Today* 1: 107–18.

13. *Chronotopes and Chronotypes*

For Bakhtin (1981), a chronotope captures something about the way in which ideas of time are projected onto space, so we can talk about mapping time or even about moving backwards and forwards in time. That idea has been generalised so that dis-cussion of multiple chronotopes offers a way of thinking about different temporalities. Although not widely taken up, we can think of chronotypes as being kinds (or *types*) of chronotopes (Harro-Loit and Köresaar 2010). Time and temporality are on my list of omitted concepts, partly because I deal with them in my study of divination, where topics such as prediction and the status of the future have to be considered. Here I will simply say that the original definition of chronotopes links time and space. It is worth considering other metaphorical resources (such as interference or haunting), and indeed it seems that the idea of the chronotope is increasingly being generalised into a way of discussing temporal configurations, how individual cultures or societies think about time. But this raises concerns about heterogeneity: what if some members of a community have different chronotopes from others (perhaps members of a particular religious persuasion)? Can there be only one chronotope per community, or culture, or society? Temporal matters are not immune from these long-standing conundrums about how we generalise about complex, diverse and heterogeneous topics. And the general ways in which we construct and use generalisations about human groups provide workable solutions enabling discussion of temporality. Any claim that such-and-such is the chronotope of that group must be treated as cautiously as any other generalisation about the group. Just as we know that differences are likely between those of different ages and different genders, so there may also be other important subdivisions, and possibly distinct minority groups whose understandings (here chronotopes) may differ significantly from those of the majority with whom they live. Ways in which people organise lives in time and think about time may not be uniform within 'a single' society. Nonetheless, chronotopes may help us understand the complexity of individual cases.

References

Bakhtin, M.M. 1981. 'Forms of Time and Chronotope in the Novel: Notes Towards a Historical Poetics', in M. Holquist (ed.), *The Dialogic Imagination: Four Essays*. Austin, TX: University of Texas Press, pp. 84–258.

Harro-Loit, H., and Köresaar, E. 2010. 'Revising Time in Cultural Research. Preface to the special issue of *Trames*', *Trames* 14: 303–6.

Zeitlyn, D. 2020. 'Haunting, Dutching and Interference: Provocations for the Anthropology of Time', *Current Anthropology* 61(4): 495–513.

14. Collage/Montage

I have described my account of the life of a senior Mambila woman as an anthropological silhouette. I found this metaphor apt and useful because it connotes the artefactuality and the art-fulness of an anthropological account. It also points to the fact that there is an empirical basis for what we say, without disguising that there is more than is ever said. The anthropological account is not and cannot be the last word on everything (I do not think that there is such an account, but that is a different matter).

Another useful metaphor for anthropology is that of collage, occurring as a contrasting pair with montage. The collage/montage distinction comes from film studies, referring to different aspects of editing. In montage, the aim is to present contrasts: for example, a split screen may show two or more scenes simultaneously, enabling and necessitating immediate comparisons. For Alan Latham, montage can be used to address the 'virtual multiplicity of the non-representational world' (2004). In Suhr and Willerslev's collection (2013), a variety of authors from different disciplines use the idea of montage to show that contrasts and edited juxtapositions are powerful techniques in contemporary anthropology, whether or not involving film. The stress on contrast means that montage encourages comparative perspectives. George Marcus in his Afterword sums this up as 'intellectual montage'.

Collage juxtaposes the contrasting scenes identified in montage by 'jarring' edits that take the viewer abruptly from one scene to another. Although a collage may be sequential, no attempt is made to obscure the editorial process that created it. The final version is left with the joins showing, so that viewers are conscious of the intervention of the editors. As Lutkehaus and Cool discuss, collage is a filmic technique that deliberately breaks the narrativity of film by 'showing the joins' (1999: 123), emphasising its artefactual and constructed qualities.

References

Latham, A. 2004. 'Research and Writing Everyday Accounts of the City: An Introduction to the Diary-Photo Diary-Interview Method', in C. Knowles and P. Sweetman (eds), *Picturing the Social Landscape: Visual Methods and the Sociological Imagination.* London: Routledge, pp. 117–31.

Lutkehaus, N., and J. Cool. 1999. 'Paradigms Lost and Found: The "Crisis of Representation" and Visual Anthropology', in J.M. Gaines and M. Renov (eds), *Collecting Visible Evidence (Visible Evidence; v. 6).* London: University of Minnesota Press, pp. 116–39.

Marcus, G.E. 2013. 'Afterword: The Traffic in Montage, Then and Now', in C. Suhr and R. Willerslev (eds), *Transcultural Montage.* New York: Berghahn Books, pp. 302–7.

Suhr, C., and R. Willerslev (eds). 2013. *Transcultural Montage.* New York: Berghahn Books.

Zeitlyn, D. 2008. 'Life History Writing and the Anthropological Silhouette', *Social Anthropology* 16(2): 154–71.

15. Colligation

Colligation is the making of connections between events; the term is now used in history and sociology to mean the teasing out of *causal* connections. A profound challenge is faced by historians, anthropologists and people just living their lives: namely, to distinguish cause from effect, in other words to distinguish correlation from causation. Whether two events share a common cause or whether one has caused another is often difficult to determine, especially at a remove of time. It may be unclear whether those events share any common cause: they may be simple coincidences. Analysis is needed, and we may have to split things up before grouping them together again. Grouping under a label is the most general meaning of colligation, and, of course, the next issue is the choice and appropriateness of the labels (sortals) used. These questions are addressed in the entry on *agnosia* (§2).

These issues raise consequent questions about what counts as evidence: how can we know whether this caused that? What sort of evidence would help us make up our mind and establish a justifiable account of what went on? This may seem abstract and academic, but it is a formalisation of a very common set of issues. Questions such as 'who broke the window?', 'who robbed the bank?', 'what caused this illness?' are, if not universal, then close to being so. As anthropologists, if we can give an account of how such questions are answered, in terms of the sorts of things adduced as evidence and the possible causes that are acceptable, then we have gone a long way to understanding what makes a particular group work. What is the local understanding of the bounds of possibility? What are the locally recognised forms of causation that must be considered when giving an account of an event?

In the context of seriousness and irony, including the controversial instance of how German historians understand the Holocaust as a case study, Michael Carrithers makes a general point about the relation of pasts to futures and how necessary it is to generalise, projecting forwards in order to live in our various mundane worlds. He says

> We not only 'live forward', but we also 'interpret forward', that is, we use abstracting concepts to grasp and communicate a view of experience beyond what is present, beyond immediacy and into the future, to tame the ramifying possibilities of what could happen and achieve a taken-for-granted understanding that is broad enough to see things as more or less predictable and reliable. (Carrithers 2012: 55)

The use of these 'abstracting concepts' is a form of colligation.

Qv: *agnosia; figuration; vignettes*

References

Carrithers, M. 2012. 'Seriousness, Irony and the Mission of Hyperbole', *Religion and Society* 3: 51–75.

Munslow, A. 2006 (1997). *Deconstructing History*, 2nd edn. Routledge: London.

Swedberg, R. 2017. 'Colligation', in H. Leiulfsrud and P. Sohlberg (eds), *Concepts in Action: Conceptual Constructionism*. Leiden: The Netherlands: Brill, pp. 63–78.

16. Commitment

The idea of commitment provides a powerful alternative to belief, meaning and truth. This notion has been developed by the
philosopher Robert Brandom. He changes the question in ways
that anthropologists and other social scientists often do, which
is part of the process of doing research. Rather than asking 'what
did they mean when they said X?' he would have us ask 'what
have they committed themselves to by saying X?' This moves us
from an abstract philosophy of language to a grounded sociology
of language use. Commitment implies an acknowledgement of
social contracts, of people with roles and relationships. This may
feel like heavy baggage for philosophers, but for anthropologists
it should be liberating, taking us back to our home turf. Even
better, the same approach works also as an alternative to truth:
for example, in argumentation theory, as in British legal practice,
the issue is not which position is true or correct but which wins
the argument, or the case in court. Brandom talks of 'the *game* of
giving and asking for reasons' (2001: 61, my emphasis).

Commitments can be tested, and when explicit they can
be challenged. However, they may be implicit, rarely becoming apparent. It can be extremely helpful for anthropologists
when implicit commitments are made explicit, emerging from
the obscurity of tacit assumption to become the spotlit focus of
discussion, and possibly argument. Moreover, it is powerful and
revealing for a comparative anthropology that different cultural
traditions have different challengeable commitments. So, unlike in Western Europe, in many places in Papua New Guinea
and in some Polynesian groups, a person's *intentions* cannot be
referred to when playing the 'reasons game'. Actions are what
matter: speakers avoid imputing intentions to others. This does
not mean they lack commitments, but the grounds for attribut-
ing and challenging them are different.

The most radical suggestion is that using commitment as an
analytic concept means that belief can be quietly dropped, or

rather left only as an object of study: it might feature as explicandum (the thing to be explained) but not as explicans (the terms of analysis).

It might be objected that a potentially infinite expansion of commitments is entailed by any utterance. That concern resembles those about affordances, where ideas of salience may similarly help remove the concerns on a pragmatic level. This also has the benefit of accommodating how understanding may vary between people: the commitments undertaken by one speaker may not be identical with those of another, even if they both make the same utterance; their understanding of the ramifications and significance of that utterance may vary (in vernacular shorthand, they attribute different meanings to it). Such differences are clearest when we contrast expert and lay uses of, for example, the names of metals: 'the metallurgist understands the concept tellurium better than I do, for training has made her master of the inferential intricacies of its employment in a way that I can only crudely approximate' (Brandom 2001: 64). This suggests a parallel with Dan Sperber's 'epidemiology of beliefs' (1990; 1996), which can also be glossed as an 'epidemiology of representations'. This sought to change how we think about the ways beliefs are held by groups: not all or nothing but with varying distributions, which have patterns (structures) that may change over time. Brandom never talks of an epidemiology of commitments, but he sometimes comes close to it: 'Grooming our concepts and material inferential commitments in the light of our assertional commitments, including those we find ourselves with noninferentially through observation, and the latter in the light of the former, is a messy, retail business' (2001: 75). Pleasingly, this suggests a contrast between anthropology and philosophy, where philosophy deals with the wholesale while anthropology is concerned with the mess of 'retail business'.

Qv: *affordance*; *argumentation theory*; *dialetheism*; *finitism*; *representation*

References

Brandom, R. 2001. *Articulating Reasons: An Introduction to Inferentialism.* Cambridge, MA: Harvard University Press.

Sperber, D. 1990. 'The Epidemiology of Beliefs', in C. Fraser and G. Gaskell (eds), *The Social Psychological Study of Widespread Beliefs.* Oxford: Clarendon Press, pp. 25–44.

———. 1996. *Explaining Culture: A Naturalistic Approach.* Oxford, Blackwell.

Taylor, C. 1992. *The Ethics of Authenticity.* Cambridge, MA: Harvard University Press.

Comparison: see *Bootstrapping*

D

Dialetheism/Paraconsistency

17. Dialetheism/Paraconsistency

Dialetheism and paraconsistency are two different ways of dealing with inconsistency. Those using paraconsistency are controlling or managing inconsistency, whereas dialetheism embraces it. Walt Whitman's poem 'Song of Myself' is dialetheistic: 'Do I contradict myself? Very well, then I contradict myself, I am large, I contain multitudes' (1892: section 51). This is where Brandom's *commitments* (§16) coupled with Sperber's epidemiology of belief /representation (1990; 1996) can be helpful: we can think of an epidemiology of commitments that maps how different commitments change over time and space, thereby capturing the way that most contradictions are not blindingly obvious. An outsider (perhaps an anthropologist) is more likely to recognise them and, by documenting and collating, to tease out and make explicit the implications of the contradictory commitments. If this never takes place, then contrary positions may remain happily in different silos. An unquestioned implicit contradiction is not 'live'. And even when a contradiction is made 'live', the conflicting commitments being actively recognised, many people will be less troubled by it than will academics who have studied philosophy, who are all too conscious that from a contradiction anything can follow. Others may shrug their shoulders and leave the problem for another day, maybe forever. Despite the fact that anything can follow from a contradiction, one may choose not to go down that path. As Lewis Carrol pointed out in his account of *What the Tortoise Said to Achilles*, there is no obligation to draw an inference, even if an inference can be drawn. For many people, everyday life is messy, and among that mess contradictions may be found. It is not the job of anthropologists to 'sort out' the contradictions. I think our task is to try to understand how contradictions have arisen and when and how they are managed. There may well be locally recognised and instituted means to resolve explicit contradictions (which may include avoiding them for a while). It may be less important whether to call such strategies para-consistency or dialetheism than to recognise them as means of making contradictions an entirely manageable part of everyday life.

Qv: *commitment*; *incommensurability*

References

Carroll, L. 1979. 'What the Tortoise said to Achilles', in D.R. Hofstadter (ed.), *Gödel, Escher, Bach: An Eternal Golden Braid*. New York: Basic Books, pp. 43–45.

Sperber, D. 1990. 'The Epidemiology of Beliefs', in C. Fraser and G. Gaskell (eds), *The Social Psychological Study of Widespread Beliefs*. Oxford: Clarendon Press, pp. 25–44.

———. 1996. *Explaining Culture: A Naturalistic Approach*. Oxford, Blackwell.

E

Ekphrasis; Emic and Etic; Epiphanies; Epistemography; Equifinality; Equivocation (Controlled Equivocation); Essentially Contested Concepts; Exaptation; Exemplars

18. Ekphrasis

Ekphrasis was originally a term for the description of non-existent works of art. These could be either mythical objects, such as Achilles' shield in *The Illiad*, or lost classical sculptures ('originally used by Greek classical rhetoricians to qualify a description with great visual content' (Ramos 2004: 147)). It has come to refer to language that describes or evokes imagery. In the philosophy of science, this is fundamental. As Ian Hacking puts it: 'In physics and much other interesting conversation we ... make representations – pictures in words' (1983: 145). He argues for a base definition of humans as Homo depictor, reflecting our universal tendency to create likenesses. This stance is provocative, particularly when applied to the problem of representation. It returns us to the classical contrast between diegesis (description of something) and exegesis (explanation of something that requires understanding it). Ekphrasis complicates the easy distinction between diegesis and exegesis. The terms of the description may be affected by our understanding, so the diegetic framing may depend on a form of exegesis. Certainly, description is not and cannot be neutral, but it is not an all or nothing exercise. Although neutrality may be impossible, it is still a worthy aspiration. We are engaged in engagement. We strive to comprehend, to display our comprehension and to explain how we came by it. Ekphrasis makes clear that all description has a theoretical basis and prevents appeals to some underlying raw or brute description. When giving a social science account, we filter our analysis through theoretical concepts and construct (more or less) abstracted models of events in such a way that connections can be made to phenomena on the ground. Are these connections different in kind from those between words on the page and the images they evoke? The concept of ekphrasis accommodates the theoretical challenges of non-verbal data and the partiality of narratives. It encourages us to see the process of anthropological analysis as one of *translation* (§57) not only between languages but also between media: verbal accounts of what has been seen or heard, visual records of a ritual, and so forth. Ekphrastic social science enables us to practise visual and narrative sensitivity in an empirically responsible fashion.

Qv: *equivocation*; *synaesthesia*; *translation*

References

Hacking, I. 1983. *Representing and Intervening: Introductory Topics in the Philosophy of Natural Science*. Cambridge: Cambridge University Press.

Ramos, M.J. 2004. 'Drawing the Lines: The Limitations of Intercultural Ekphrasis', in S. Pink, L. Kurti and A.I. Alfonso (eds), *Working Images: Visual Research and Representation in Ethnography*. London: Routledge, pp. 147–56.

Zeitlyn, D. 2014. 'Antinomies of Representation: Anthropology as an Ekphrastic Process', *Hau: Journal of Ethnographic Theory* 4: 341–62.

19. Emic and Etic

The contrasting terms emic and etic reflect the distinction in linguistics between phonemics (distinctions that a language recognises as meaningful) and phonetics (the sounds that humans can make, from which each language uses a subset). This contrast was developed as the cultural version of the linguistic distinction (originally by Kenneth Pike in 1954, see Headland, Pike and Harris 1990). It is emphatically *not* a gloss on, nor an academic version of, the subjective *vs.* objective distinction. The terms emic and etic are equally intersubjective. Within linguistics, phonetics is the study of the sounds made by the human voice. Phonemics looks at the subset of these sounds that distinguish different words in a language. There is dramatic variation between languages. For example, some groups of languages more or less ignore differences in tone/pitch, while others use the same differences to distinguish between words and to signal grammatical features. The cultural parallel is to say that an individual cultural system uses a particular subset of features from the wide variety available. Within the cultural system, these may be more or less explicit and may set the terms of debate with that society. They are intersubjective: shared by all the participants of that society. This is why I am so adamant against mapping the emic/etic distinction onto that between subjectivity and objectivity. To understand a society on its own terms, we must understand the emic perspective. In order to compare one society with another, which might use a very different set of emic understandings of the world, we have to adopt some sort of etic perspective. However, Mattei Candea gives a different account of comparison that complicates the matter nicely: his idea of lateral comparison juxtaposes two different emic systems, without the need for an etic *tertium quid* or neutral position.

References

Candea, M. 2019. *Comparison in Anthropology: The Impossible Method*. Cambridge: Cambridge University Press.

Headland, T.N., K.L. Pike and M. Harris. 1990. *Emics and Etics: The Insider/Outsider Debate*. London: Sage Publications.

20. Epiphanies

Norman Denzin, writing on the life histories of recovering al-
coholics, uses the idea of epiphanic moments, points at which a
life course changes direction (1989: 70–73). The idea has broad
application and connects with key transitions between different life stages, which Mandelbaum calls *turnings* (1973). These
epiphanic moments can be central to the ways in which people
create life stories (whether about themselves or others). Beyond life history, the idea has wider application: through ideas
such as critical events (Das 1995) or even cataclysmic events
(Feuchtwang 2000) in social histories we can identify links, not
only to extended case studies but also to ways of understanding
change and transition. On this account, a vignette of a critical
event may be discussed as a form of social epiphany.

Epiphanic moments may characterise and structure how
individuals understand their own lives or how a social group
views its history. They may also characterise the process of undertaking research and can be a useful means of conveying its
results. Anthropologists and many other researchers use their
involvement in the lives of the communities they are studying as a central research method, part of how they learn about
these communities. We may abruptly come to realise that our
behaviour has been wrong and that the locally appropriate way
to behave is different. This realisation can be written up and
described as an epiphanic moment in research. An extreme and
celebrated instance is Renato Rosaldo's account of grief, anger
and headhunting among the Ilongot people in northern Luzon,
Philippines. Following the tragic death of Michelle Rosaldo after she fell off a hillside path into a ravine, Renato came to
understand the emotive force of the connections between grief
and headhunting that he had been told about over several years
of research. As readers, we can better share that understanding through the use of rupture in the narrative account. The
researcher's epiphany can, to some extent, be shared with the
readers.

Qv: *vignettes*; *life writing*; *isolarion*

References

Das, V. 1995. *Critical Events: An Anthropological Perspective on Contemporary India*. Oxford, Oxford University Press.

Denzin, N.K. 1989. *Interpretive Biography*. London, Sage.

Feuchtwang, S. 2000. 'Reinscriptions: Commemoration, Restoration and the Interpersonal', in S. Radstone (ed.), *Memory and Methodology*. Oxford: Berg Publishers, pp. 59–77.

Mandelbaum, D.G. 1973. 'The Study of Life History: Gandhi', *Current Anthropology* 14: 177–206.

Rosaldo, R. 1993. 'Grief and the Headhunter's Rage', in *Culture & Truth: The Remaking of Social Analysis*. London: Routledge, pp. 167–77.

21. Epistemography

The meaning of ethnography can be glossed as 'writing about ethnic groups', and epistemography can similarly be understood as 'writing about epistemological formations', broadly covering science studies and related fields. As Peter Dear puts it: 'Epistemography is the endeavour that attempts to investigate science "in the field"' (2001: 130). Epistemology is conventionally contrasted with ontology, and perhaps epistemography has its pair in ontography. Martin Holbraad pioneered (2012) the use of the term ontography in anthropology, although it should be noted that Ian Bogost (2012) traces it back to M.R. James in the nineteenth century. For Holbraad, 'what distinguishes ontography from arbitrary ontological speculation, is the method of extrapolating analytic abstractions from the ethnographic material, rather than, say, heaping Western philosophical concepts upon it' (2012: 87). I find this sort of neologising sometimes helpful, and sometimes less so. Inventing a term can help focus the attention and provide analytic purchase. Or it may only redescribe a problem without increasing our understanding of what is going on. My advice about theoretical neologisms is to use them with great caution, and only after having considered whether another fitting term is already available. Sometimes it is better to use only a small set of analytic terms: in that case, if a new one is to be added we should consider which one might be dropped.

References

Bogost, I. 2012. 'Ontography', in *Alien Phenomenology, or What it's Like to be a Thing*. Minneapolis: University of Minnesota Press.

Dear, P. 2001. 'Science Studies as Epistemography', in J.A. Labinger and H.M. Collins (eds), *The One Culture?: A Conversation About Science*. London: University of Chicago Press, pp. 128–41.

Holbraad, M. 2012. 'Truth Beyond Doubt: Ifá oracles in Havana', *HAU: Journal of Ethnographic Theory* 2: 81–109.

Ergodicity: see *Non-ergodicity*

Etic: see *Emic and Etic*

22. Equifinality

Equifinality suggests that more than one route to the current state of affairs would have been possible. The past is no more determinate than the future. Equifinality encourages us to consider more carefully the contingency of the pasts we invoke as we move into uncertain futures. So, to change tense and ruin a popular song (*Que Será Será*), it is *not* the case that 'what will have been, was'. The 'thin red line' (TRL) of actuality threads its way through the myriad 'roads not taken': the possible worlds created by choices not made and options avoided. It seems that past possibles are impossible in that they did not happen, and that what happened therefore retrospectively becomes a necessity. In other words, it feels as if having arrived where we are our arriving here was inevitable. This is wrong in that it ignores all the other possible destinations that we avoided with each choice we made. (This is yet another reason not to trust our feelings.) Many philosophers see the TRL as leading only to the present, not extending into the future. For them, it threads backwards only. However, equifinality blurs that line: more accurately, it makes us think about the many possible lines leading to the now and then diverging into the futures ahead of us. Adopting the idea of equifinality changes how we consider making and writing history and how we 'mine the past'. The biggest problem in considering possible pasts and possible futures is assessing what is or was possible. We may be prepared to discuss possible worlds but fewer will countenance impossible worlds. The issue then is: who determines whether a world is possible or impossible? What criteria could or should be used? Who is to say what was possible? However we resolve these conundrums, it seems clear that when we change our understanding of the past our understanding of the course of the TRL also changes. Thus the past may not be as unchanging as it appears.

Bernard Lategan builds on Koselleck's focus on the interaction of experience and expectation to argue that sense-making (of or about the past) has a future orientation (2010: 147). He accords ontological priority not to the real but to the possible. This opens up connections between pasts and futures: 'It is exactly when events do *not* follow the anticipated course or do *not* comply with the expectations of common (that is, historical) wisdom, that the future potential of history becomes visible' (151, his emphases). An open future is assured by emphasising past possibles, rather than the real (in his words, stressing the 'priority of the possible' 2010: 152). This break with determinism has its own problems: who is to say what was possible? It allows him to 'remember with the future in mind' (2010: 157–58). 'The contrast between possible and not possible is not determined by the past or by what already exists. It therefore has the capacity to deal both with risk and with what is new' (2010:

158). Consequently, we must revise our idea of 'the TRL': either blurring the line so it becomes a ribbon of possible worlds, or relativistically dropping the definite article so that each viewpoint has its own TRL. Admittedly, both alternatives are difficult. On one hand is the problem of assessing what is possible, and on the other are problems relating to intersubjectivity. But the advantage of equifinality, as Lategan argues, is that it urges us to recognise the future inflection of history.

Qv: *finitism*; *non-ergodic*

References

'Equifinality', Wikipedia. Retrieved 9 October 2021 from https://en.wikipe dia.org/wiki/Equifinality.

Koselleck, R., and K. Tribe. 2004 (1985). *Futures Past: On the Semantics of Historical Time*. New York: Columbia University Press.

Lategan, B. 2010. 'Remembering with the Future in Mind', in M. Diawara, B.C. Lategan and J. Rüsen (eds), *Historical Memory in Africa: Dealing with the Past, Reaching for the Future in an Intercultural Context*. Oxford: Berghahn Books, pp. 145–61.

23. Equivocation (Controlled Equivocation)

Equivocation, especially controlled equivocation, is Viveiros de Castro's encapsulation of the exercise of translation and the juggling involved in doing anthropology (2004: 10). Controlled equivocation is about *not* trying to resolve the contradictions inherent in thinking about the world in different ways at one time. Using different languages actually often makes the task easier, but some people think very differently in different contexts despite using versions of the same language. This can be hard to describe. Viveiros de Castro encourages us to sit, uneasily or uncomfortably, in the spaces between belonging and not belonging, understanding perhaps a little, sometimes more than others. This can place us in an odd position: we cannot fully concur with those we work with to undertake our research, nor do we want to overtly disagree with them. In such circumstances, 'controlled equivocation' offers a way of managing *partiality* (§45) and incompleteness (as does *bifocal ethnography*, §8). One way to do this is to treat the alternatives as *incommensurable* (§33) and refuse to judge between them.

The comparative method or perspective, which has been key for anthropology, has implications that are relevant here. We are forced into irony and detachment, not because of neo-colonial condescension or the suggestion that 'our' science is better than 'their' superstition, but because of our refusal or inability to choose one over another: 'they can't all be right when they make mutually incompatible/contradictory claims about the world'. The situation of bad faith in which we are placed may be uncomfortable, but so too is commitment to a single ontology.

Fredrik Barth is perhaps an extreme case, since he worked in so many locations around the world. If he had taken seriously the injunction to take other views seriously (Viveiros de Castro 2011: 133), then consider the number of things to which he would (really, really) have to adhere. A list of his fieldwork locations (Barth 2007) serves as a proxy for the different ontologies associated with the sociocultural traditions found there:

Norway
Bali
Sudan (Darfur)
Papua New Guinea (Baktaman)
Iran (Basseri tribe of the Khamseh Confederacy)
Pakistan (Swat Pathans)
Oman (Sohar).

Of course, his knowledge of each society is less profound than a lifetime there would have allowed; of course, his understanding is incomplete (as is everyone's). But if we accept that he knows something about each of these highly disparate places, then his head encompasses many ontologies. Viveiros de Castro suggests that a form of controlled equivocation is a way of managing the cognitive dissonance, and of arriving at perhaps surprising understandings through the juxtapositions at play.

Qv: *ironic detachment; incommensurability; partiality; translation*

References

Barth, F. 2007. 'Overview: Sixty Years in Anthropology', *Annual Review of Anthropology* 36: 1–16.

Viveiros De Castro, E. 2004. 'Perspectival Anthropology and the Method of Controlled Equivocation', *Tipití: Journal of the Society for the Anthropology of Lowland South America* 2: 3–22.

———. 2011. 'Zeno and the Art of Anthropology', *Common Knowledge* 17: 128–45.

Zeitlyn, D. 2014. 'Lévy-Bruhl and Ontological Déjà vu: An Appendix to Vigh and Sausdal', *Journal of the Anthropological Society of Oxford* 6(2): 213–17.

24. Essentially Contested Concepts

Essentially contested concepts are to conceptual structures what *wicked problems* (§60) are to planning and coordinated action. Gallie (1956) discusses 'appraisive concepts', and after a hypothetical example from team sports, he discusses religious affiliation (in his example, 'being a good Christian'), democracy and art. His examples show that evaluative ideologies lurk at the edges of what can also be claimed to be neutral classificatory decisions: this is perhaps clearest in disputes about whether a work is or is not 'art'. The status of Duchamp's porcelain urinal, re-purposed as the found-art piece 'Fountain', illustrates the dilemma. Gallie's hypothetical example now reads as a parallel to Wittgenstein's well known discussion of family resemblance, which also uses games to argue against forms of essentialism. Gallie's conclusion is that 'it is quite impossible to find a *gen-*

eral principle for deciding which of two contestant uses of an essentially contested concept really "uses it best"' (1956: 189, his emphasis). If people have different understandings of words like 'art', 'freedom' and 'democracy', then they are condemned at best to argue across each other. Mieke Bal considers these issues by reference to 'travelling concepts', arguing that it is unwise to be overly concerned with definitional exactitude: part of the point of travelling is that meanings shift (see *finitism*, §29). She advocates for acceptance of mess and points out that confusion can be productive. In other words, we can overdo concerns about conceptual precision. To rephrase Gallie's argument, the concepts in question are what Susan Leigh Star called *'boundary objects'* (§10): concepts that span divides and provide the substance of debate, argument and division. As such they are, or should be, the explicanda, not the explanans. Indeed, as Gallie argues, it would be a category mistake to think that the problems can be resolved by finally arriving at a perfectly definitive definition. Since definitional issues are tied up with political entanglements, consensus cannot be achieved. As analysts, we should pick explanatory or analytic terms that are less contentious and seek to understand the arguments in more prosaic and knowingly incomplete ways. As far as possible, the terms of analysis should not be essentially contested. This leaves room for the political and other uses of the words at issue, which is entirely appropriate for them. The result might be a sparser anthropology, but it will be clearer than is currently usual about what is being explored, in what terms and to what purposes.

Qv: *boundary objects*; *finitism*; *wicked problems*

References

Bal, M. 2002. *Travelling Concepts in the Humanities: A Rough Guide*. Toronto, University of Toronto Press.

Gallie, W.B. 1956. 'Essentially Contested Concepts', *Proceedings of the Aristotelian Society* 56: 167–98.

25. Exaptation

Exaptation is Stephen Jay Gould and Elizabeth Vrba's term for the process whereby 'structures that may have evolved for one purpose are co-opted for quite different functions for which they happen to come in handy' (Ingold 1997: 119). Gould and Vrba were writing as biologists, but Tim Ingold applies the idea to artefacts and language. Adaption is always a process of exaptation, whereby something is changed by being adapted. Ingold argues for a contrasting pair: 'ex-aptation and ad-aptation'. The range of possible uses depends on the affordances possessed by the thing or structure. The idea of repurposing and transformation by reuse in different contexts encourages us to recognise indeterminacy and openness, which in turn fosters humility. It is also worth noting that Ingold's use is itself an instance of the idea: the model from biological evolution is applied to cultural phenomena never considered by the originators. We could consider Richard Dawkins' notorious invention of the meme to be another such case, repurposing the idea of the gene in a cultural context and neologising in the process.

Qv: *affordance*; *finitism*

Reference

Ingold, T. 1997. 'Eight Themes in the Anthropology of Technology', *Social Analysis* 41: 106–38.

26. Exemplars

Social science uses exemplars in three ways. The first is as a means of resolving the conundrum that the problems of radical *translation* (§57) identified by Quine seem not to apply in practice. Translation, especially translation-as-interpretation, poses no practical problem in everyday life. In effect, the philosophical problems are *assumed* not to bite. In Quine's hypothetical case, the language learner cannot tell whether a term applies to a rabbit or just to a 'rabbit-part'. Eleanor Rosch's work resolves this conundrum. Considering objects of the scale with which humans interact, she found evidence that people treat them as 'basic level objects' (Rosch et al. 1976; Rosch 1977). The concept of basic level objects provides a justification for a default translation of Quine's uncertain term as 'rabbit', rather than 'rabbit-part', although such justification is rarely called for, if ever. These 'basic level objects' can serve as exemplars when we make translations, or we could say that they act as *boundary objects* (§10) in multilingual interactions.

In a different context, Thomas Kuhn talked of exemplars as a way of clarifying his discussion of paradigms in science. For him, exemplars are models or templates that help when thinking about new problems. They can be boundary objects, linking disparate fields, where each field understands the exemplar differently but by agreeing on the exemplar users can avoid direct conflict about these differences.

The third use of exemplars is as anti-essentialist alternatives to definition (discussed at greater length in the entries on *ostension* (§42) and *vignettes* (§59)). Here exemplars are used to demonstrate standard, common instances of a term, leaving the learner to infer and then test through usage the range of meanings to which the term can be applied. And since meanings are not exhausted by past usage, there will always be a residue of uncertainty about appropriate usage. This positions flexibility and the possibility of creative reworkings at the heart of the use of exemplars.

Qv: *boundary objects; finitism; ostension; translation; vagueness*

References

Kuhn, T.S. 1962. *The Structure of Scientific Revolutions.* Chicago, IL: Chicago University Press.

Rosch, E., C.B. Mervis, W.D. Gray, D.M. Johnson, and P. Boyes-Braem. 1976. 'Basic Objects in Natural Categories', *Cognitive Psychology* 8: 382–439.

Rosch, E.M. 1977. 'Classification of Real-World Objects: Origins and Representations in Cognition', in P.N. Johnson-Laird and P.C. Wilson (eds), *Thinkings: Readings in Cognitive Science*. Cambridge: Cambridge University Press, pp. 212–22.

F

Faithfulness; Figuration; Finitism (Meaning Finitism); Forbearing and 'Subjective Counterfactuals'

27. Faithfulness

Faithfulness can do much of the work often given to truth. By this, I mean that we have to do very similar work whether we are judging an account to be *faithful* or *true*. Faithfulness can also, at least in part, replace the idea of representation in concepts such as faithful characterisations (see Just and Zeitlyn 2014). Consideration of faithfulness can be fruitful, prompting questions such as 'faithful *in what respect* or *for what purpose*', moving us beyond all-or-nothing dichotomising. Rather than having to choose between good and bad, or true and false, we can deal with a continuum: we can aspire to make our accounts better rather than worse but always in a matter of degree. As Andrew Brandel and Marco Motta ask '"What is it to describe a form of life? And how are we to do such a thing with tact?" The question of the "rightness" of description then emerges as related to the question of what exactly it is "to give a realistic account of the lives of others"' (2021: 19). Their idea of tactful description is similar to Wittgenstein's 'perspicuous presentation' (2018: 46), where opinions may vary dramatically about what is tactful or perspicuous. The inevitability of *detachment* (§36), *equivocation* (§23) and the ironic stance of anthropological accounts set some limits to aspirations to faithfulness and make fraught our attempts at tactfulness. *Agnosia* (§2) raises other concerns: we may not understand what we are talking about (in the visual example in the agnosia entry, we may not see what we are looking at). Anthropologists give accounts that anticipate comparison, and these also push the bounds of faith-fulness: being faithful in one instance might have entailments incompatible with another case, making inevitable some form of *ironic detachment* (§36).

What might 'keeping faith' mean for an anthropologist? It can mean different things at different times and is none the worse for this. During and after fieldwork, one has a responsi-bility to people with whom one has spent time to keep faith in a human, personal way. But one also has wider responsibilities that can conflict with this duty. Being faithful to the under-standing enabled by fieldwork may mean saying and publishing things that the community in question would rather not have trumpeted abroad. Here the limited readership of most aca-demic publishing, even in the age of social media, gives some protection. But to say as an absolute principle that the com-munity's views are paramount would render it impossible for any researcher to study anything troubling: from malnutrition to domestic violence and sex-selective abortion. Academic re-searchers are pulled in multiple directions by calls to be faithful to conflicting ideals and to conflicting positions. I think it is better to identify and acknowledge these conflicts than to aim for and cling to a single (impossibly ideal) position.

Qv: *agnosia; ironic detachment; equivocation; wicked problems*

References

Brandel, A., and M. Motta. 2021. 'Introduction: Life with Concepts', in A. Brandel and M. Motta (eds), *Living with Concepts: Anthropology in the Grip of Reality*. New York: Fordham University Press, pp. 1–28.

Just, R., and D. Zeitlyn. 2014. *Excursions in Realist Anthropology: A Merological Approach*. Newcastle upon Tyne: Cambridge Scholars Publishing.

Wittgenstein, L. (Translated by S. Palmié) 2018. 'Remarks on Frazer's The Golden Bough', in G. Da Col and S. Palmié (eds), *The Mythology in Our Language: Remarks on Frazer's Golden Bough*. Chicago: Hau Books, pp. 29–73.

28. Figuration

Figuration is Norbert Elias' way of resisting sociological individualism: the idea that individual humans are the atoms of society and that these are the only things that matter. It is another means of talking about structures and social features that shape and constrain people, whose actions create and reproduce those structures, changing them as they go. For example, a game or dance can be characterised independently of the participating individuals that 'actualise' (or 'achieve') a performance. In short, generalisation IS possible! And if the people concerned talk about games and dances in which they participate or make implicit distinctions between them (as well as explicit ones), then there is justification for the identification of units, the drawing of lines that divide parts of the intrinsically connected *Hesse net* (§32) that links the concepts involved.

Generalising beyond units or groupings, Elias used figuration to talk about social roles, which are separate from and not exhausted by the individuals who occupy them (so resembling the players of games). Identifying people as occupying the same role, playing the same game, is a form of grouping under a label: one aspect of *colligation* (§15). This is important in *positioning theory* (§47), where these figurations are called positions, meaning the social roles occupied by participants in a social process or event. In distinguishing between roles or positions and the occupants, making generalisations that leave out the idiosyncrasies of individuals and events, we must come to terms with the random *stochastic variations* (§53) and, despite the noise this produces, perform the figuration summarised in an account of a game, dance or social role.

Qv: *colligation*; *Hesse nets*; *positioning theory*; *stochastic variation*

References

Dunning, E. and J. Hughes. 2013. *Norbert Elias and Modern Sociology*. London: Bloomsbury Academic.

Rebel, H. 2005. 'Figurations in Historical Anthropology: Two Kinds of Structural Narrative about Long-Duration Provenances of the Holocaust', in D. Kalb and H. Tak (eds), *Critical Junctions: Anthropology and History Beyond the Cultural Turn*. Oxford: Berghahn Books, pp. 72–87.

Stanley, L. 2015. 'The Scriptural Economy, the Forbes Figuration and the Racial Order: Everyday Life in South Africa 1850–1930', *Sociology* 49: 837–52.

29. Finitism (Meaning Finitism)

The argument behind the notion of meaning finitism is that any present usage of a term (concept or idea) is underdetermined by past usage. Contrasting with a potentially infinite number of future uses of a term, there have only been a finite number of past uses. Meanings are not entirely established by the past: they become established by *ostension* (§42) and often by *exemplar* (§26). There is always the possibility of future shifts in meaning, which renders present usage uncertain, let alone future usage. Philosophy of science seems to find this more worrying than anthropology and other social sciences, where the idea of incremental alteration (creeping shifts in the meaning, orientation or function of a social feature: see *exaptation*, §25) seems to be a reasonable characterisation of social change. Instead of meaning finitism, perhaps we should be considering social finitism or societal finitism: the ways in which one generation live their lives do not exhaust (fully determine) how other generations will live theirs.

David Leung uses finitism in his exploration of *The Sociology of Financial Reporting and Auditing* (his subtitle). He builds on the five implications of finitism identified by the philosophers of science Barry Barnes, David Bloor and John Henry.

These implications are that: '1. the future applications of terms are open-ended; 2. no act of classification is ever indefeasibly correct; 3. all acts of classification are revisable; 4. successive applications of a kind term are not independent; and 5. the applications of different kind terms are not independent of each other' (Leung 2016: 7). This suggests that flexibility and adaptability are possible because of the inescapability of an element of *vagueness* (§58).

Q*v*: *essentially contested concepts*; *equifinality*; *commitments*; *Hesse nets*; *instauration*; *ostension*; *vagueness*

References

Bal, M. 2002. *Travelling Concepts in the Humanities: A Rough Guide*. Toronto: University of Toronto Press.

Leung, D. 2016. *Inside Accounting: The Sociology of Financial Reporting and Auditing*. London, Routledge.

30. Forbearing and 'Subjective Counterfactuals'

Forbearing (synonymous with withholding) concerns choices to act. This includes decisions *not* to act, which are equally active decisions. There are a near infinite number of acts that I have chosen not to do, mainly by inadvertence, but often following from some previous action. As noted above, the idea of *affordances* (§1) seems to be imperilled or *infirmed* (§34) if we cannot list the possible uses of an object. Similarly, if I cannot list the action choices or forbearances I have made, then how useful is this idea? The narratives we tell about ourselves and the world are full of such forbearances: the time I said 'no'; the occasion when I chose to travel by bus rather than walk. We map out the consequences of our actions in the stories we tell ourselves and others. Indeed, we live in worlds full of wonder, worlds full of possibility, worlds filled with unrealised possibles. It is a wonder we don't choke on them. We move on by recognising them briefly and then putting them out of mind, concentrating on the concrete: the field we are actually planting by hand rather than the possible other field we would have been cultivating with machinery had the mean anthropologist provided the money to buy a tractor. Dwelling on such possibilities, including what would have happened had we not acted (had we chosen to forebear), can take us to subjective counterfactuals: 'actors reasoning about what would have happened if they had forborne to act in certain ways' (Abell 2004: 296).

Qv: *affordance*

Reference

Abell, P. 2004. 'Narrative Explanation: An Alternative to Variable-Centered Explanation?', *Annual Review of Sociology* 30: 287–310.

Gobbets: see *Vignettes*

H

Hapax; Hesse Nets

31. Hapax

A hapax (strictly hapax legomenon) is a one-off occurrence. The term comes from classical studies and refers to words with one single attested instance. All fieldwork is unique and unrepeatable, and so by extension it could be called a hapax, as could internet research: since the online world is in constant flux, it is impossible to repeat research in exactly the same circumstances. Anthropology as an empirical fieldworking discipline is a celebration of the generalisability of hapatic phenomena. Because humans create and recognise categories, we tend to gloss over differences that we deem inconsequential. In so doing, we link different unique events that we see as instances of the 'same' type (*colligating* (§15) them as *figurations* (§28)). We construct kinds as we construct our worlds (although not entirely in terms of our own choosing: external factors can provide strong constraints).

Like much anthropology, this resembles Philip Runkel's 'method of specimens' (discussed in the entry on *vignettes*, §59). Anthropologists often deal with a 'sample of one'. The lesson is that an individual case can have wide significance, despite its quirky or unusual features, and possibly because of them. As Carlo Ginzburg has argued, discussing micro history, concentrating on one individual is a way to comprehend the world. Ginzburg says that 'a life chosen at random can make concretely visible the attempt to unify the world, as well as some of its implications (2005: 682). Indeed, an individual and their life can serve as ... starting points, for concrete details from which the global process can be inductively reconstructed' (2005: 666). We can learn many wider lessons by concentrating on the details of single cases, whether we call them vignettes, microhistory case studies or ethnographic biographies.

Qv: *catachresis*; *figuration*; *non-ergodic*; *prosopography*; *vignettes*

References

Ginzburg, C. 2005. 'Latitude, Slaves, and the Bible: An Experiment in Microhistory'. *Critical Inquiry* 31(3): 665–83.
Runkel, P.J. 1990. *Casting Nets and Testing Specimens: Two Grand Methods of Psychology*. New York: Praeger Publishers.

32. Hesse Nets

Hesse nets are nets of meaning. The idea, from the philosopher of science Mary Hesse, captures the way that any one concept is connected to many (all) others, so that changing one affects them all. This is a nice idea but easily exaggerated. Nets can have holes, and the constraining or altering effects diminish with distance (and contentiously with modularity) so that some parts of a conceptual system may be relatively insulated from others. In principle, everything may indeed be connected to everything else, but in practice some parts may change without any apparent effect on other distant parts of the net.

The sorts of semantic mapping that result from argument mapping, textual analysis or even mapping the patterns of cross-references in a book such as this are examples of Hesse nets. When I anticipated creating such a diagram for this book (now part of the Introduction), I was unsure which concepts would occupy its centre by virtue of being connected to the most other entries. I thought that *affordance* (§1), *vagueness* (§58) and perhaps *translation* (§57) would be central but not that other items such as *finitism* (§29) might turn out to be near the core of the intermeshed conceptual network. The surprises following from creation of the diagram and the re-evaluation that followed are among the benefits of undertaking network analysis to identify the actual (rather than imagined) reticulations of a Hesse net. (Note that I have not included the terms just mentioned in the network of cross-references.)

Having generated the diagram, I was surprised by its revelation of the importance not only of finitism but also of colligation, figuration and ostension. Although these concepts were not salient in my mind, the diagram shows that they serve as bridges between parts of the network that would otherwise be unconnected. In the jargon of network analysis, they have 'betweenness centrality', even if they do not appear in the literal centre of the diagram.

Qv: *figuration; repleteness*

Reference

Hesse, M.B. 1974. *The Structure of Scientific Inference.* Berkeley: University of California Press.

I

Incommensurability; Infirming; Instauration; Ironic Detachment; Irrealism; Isolarion

Immutable Mobiles: see *Boundary Objects*

33. Incommensurability

There is a fundamental contradiction in the idea of deciding that two positions are incommensurable. For, in order to make the judgment, one must in some sense have comprehended them both and perhaps been able to compare if not 'co-measure' them. In that sense, any judgment that two things are incommensurable includes a self-contradictory judgment that they are commensurable. Thinking in many different ways is common among humans. The differences and impossibilities have been exaggerated. We are not prisoners of our ways of thought, as some have suggested: otherwise that suggestion could not have been made.

Eva Spies uses incommensurability as a way of comprehending in the world while avoiding binary judgments. For her:

> With the concept of incommensurability, we attempt to come to terms with situations in which people do not appear to refer to a common frame of reference and do not feel the need for one practice or view to include or exclude another. Sometimes different ways of doing and seeing things do not stand with or against another – they simply stand side by side. (2013: 123)

On this account, the important thing about incommensurability is the *not*-judging. We must recognise a potential *aporia* (§3) in that it may be impossible to choose between two views, perspectives or ways of being in the world. More importantly, it may not be necessary to choose between them at all: there is no need to form a judgment. Nurit Bird-David's *bifocality* (§8) and Viveiros de Castro's *controlled equivocation* (§23) are other ways of considering this issue: balancing or juggling the different sets of ideas one is struggling to comprehend, however imperfectly. This enables us to 'communicate by differences instead of silencing the Other by presuming a univocality – the essential similarity – between what the Other and We are saying' (2004: 10).

So incommensurability encourages acceptance of multiplicity, even though this may be hard to achieve in everyday life. Acceptance of conflicting positions is easier for academics than for people obliged to make decisions outside of ivory towers. Deciding whether or not I should be vaccinated can affect my own health and that of those around me. This sort of decision has a path dependency. Equivocating about whether to have a vaccination or not may be taken as an analogue to the way that beliefs about illness can be treated as incommensurable. However, despite the connections between the two, the act of vaccination (or its withholding) cannot be: one cannot undo the action and regain the state of being unvaccinated. We need to be clear that any putative incommensurability applies, not to actions (or withholdings) but to the explanations (narratives) given to explain and justify our decisions.

Qv: *aporia*; *bifocality*; *equivocation*

References

Spies, E. 2013. 'Coping with Religious Diversity: Incommensurability and Other Perspectives', in B. Janice and L. Michael (eds), *A Companion to the Anthropology of Religion*. London: Wiley, pp. 118–36.

Viveiros de Castro, E. 2004. Perspectival Anthropology and the Method of
    Controlled Equivocation. *Tipití: Journal of the Society for the Anthropology
    of Lowland South America* 2(1): 3–22.

Incompleteness: see *Partiality*

Indeterminacy: see *Vagueness*

34. Infirming

Infirming is an antonym for confirming. This is useful when
discussing case studies and their relationship to theory. While
some cases may be taken as confirming a theoretical position,
others may infirm it, raising questions about its ability to provide an explanatory framework for events in the worlds that
people inhabit. Anthropology has often found problems with
models imported from stereotypical hard science; for example,
nomothetical models (theory/prediction/testing) and even the
Popperian mantra of seeking refutation rather than proof. Infirming can be seen as a weaker form of refutation: if an instance infirms a theory, then at the very least it casts doubt on
or raises questions about that theory. For example, in the entry
on *affordances* (§1) the possibly infinite lists of an object's possible uses could be seen as infirming the concept of affordance.
If we accept the idea of confirming, shouldn't we also accept
infirming?

35. Instauration

Instauration is a clever expression of some of the ways in which
people make bridges between pasts and presents, or how they

enable innovation and new uses by saying that what they are doing is well established or even traditional. Karin Barber uses the idea when talking about how texts are used in different circumstances across time.

> With texts, people perform what you might call (using an old Elizabethan term) acts of 'instauration', that is, 'institution, founding, establishment' but also 'restoration, renovation, renewal' (OED). People innovatively establish social forms and attentively maintain them; both the establishment and the maintenance are creative, emergent and continuous. Texts, in this view, are instances of instauration which are central to human experience. (Barber 2007: 4)

This is a way of thinking about re-creation, of a continuous redefining, which has been ongoing for millennia. It affords another way of approaching Bergson's view of time as duration. Instauration is about both instituting/creating *and* restoring/renewing. What tense does this concept then require? It is a way of thinking across or amidst time.

An example of such a process, for which I am grateful to Michael Carrithers, is the way in which twentieth-century forest monks in Sri Lanka re/established (or re/created) a way of life that we might see as being 'stamped with the ancient' but that actually varies greatly from one instauration to another.

Bruno Latour popularised another sense of instauration, originally from Étienne Souriau, for whom it bridges language and understanding: this denotes the imaginative leap between sculptor and sculpture, or potter and clay, as the craftsperson comes to realise (mainly by feel) what it is they are making; this is an almost entirely embodied sort of deictic connection.

Qv: *finitism*

References

Barber, K. 2007. *The Anthropology of Texts, Persons and Publics: Oral and Written Culture in Africa and Beyond*. Cambridge: Cambridge University Press.

Latour, B. 2011. 'Reflections on Etienne Souriau's Les Modes d'existence', in G. Harman, L. Bryant, L. and N. Srnicek (eds), *The Speculative Turn: Continental Materialism and Realism*. Melbourne: re.press, pp. 304–33.

36. Ironic Detachment

Anthropologists conducting fieldwork can find themselves in an odd relationship to the people they are living with. For they are *both* the ultimate sceptics, believing nothing they are told, and credulous fools, believing everything.

In the field, anthropologists have to do more than suspend belief (or disbelief). They sit (sometimes extremely uncomfortably) between poles, between ways of living, reflecting and accounting for actions. To accept the discomfort is to accept elements of bad faith, but it does not require relativism. The ideal is to turn this dual stance into a methodology.

The irony of this is that neither realist nor relativist anthropologists can escape from profound disagreement with those among whom they work, those they are trying to understand. Relativism provides no comfort to those who aspire to an ideal of liberal sympathy between humans. The practice of anthropology inevitably puts anthropologists in situations of more or less ironic detachment. The inevitability of this means that the discipline should accept it and that we should think about how to manage it rather than pretending that it does not happen. Working across cultural differences creates moral dilemmas as well as epistemological and ontological ones. Better to accept and deal with them as real dilemmas than to adopt a position (strong relativism) that while seeming to remove the dilemmas casts the possibility of communication into doubt. Also relevant is the argument of Erving Goffman (1959) that by present-

ing themselves differently in different situations everyone is in
a similar position, so that, in effect, that is the human condition. We should deal with it rather than seek an unachievable
consistency.

One of the few general lessons this teaches is that different
social groups, at different moments in time, and in different
places, give radically different accounts of the world and what
it is like to be human in it. Many are radically incompatible,
which leads to the quandary of anthropology: we cannot be
faithful to all our informants at once. This, more than anything
else, puts anthropology in an odd position. I contend that it is
more honest (albeit more uncomfortable) to accept this rather
than to try to relativise anthropological accounts to the norms
of any one set of people. Of course, our accounts are biased and
relative. Relative to what? To the discipline of anthropology.

One example among many is Gilbert Lewis's analysis of
Gnau female puberty rituals (1980) in which he discusses Gnau
denials that the rituals relate to (or coincide with, in the most
neutral phrasing) the onset of menstruation. Lewis analysed
the puberty rituals from a position of bad faith by continuing
to consider menstruation in his analysis of the ritual, but he
did this knowingly and openly, acknowledging that he had discussed this with many Gnau people who had disagreed with
him and denied any connection between the ritual and menstruation. To a large extent, disagreement is an aspect of the
human condition. To suggest that an account may be given
without any sort of bad faith is as naïve as suggesting there is
a wholly neutral 'god's-eye view'. As the philosopher Thomas
Nagel says, 'it should not surprise us if objectivity is essentially
incomplete' (1980: 84).

Irrespective of one's stance on the above, one could in principle adopt a position of methodological relativism. Anthropologists hold that some form of perspectivism is required when
undertaking fieldwork. We go to the field not to argue with

people (although in some cultural traditions arguing is expected
of competent adults: it is how they declare themselves as actors) but to try to understand *their* understandings of the world.
Sometimes our struggle for understanding is helped by confron-
tation and argument, but most of the time it is not. We are not
missionaries trying to convince, nor are we candidates for con-
version (to the exclusion of our previous positions). In this, an
uncomfortable and perilous middle ground, we are continually
open to accusations of bad faith (at the very least). Discomfort,
awareness of conflicting positions and uncertainty are part of
the anthropological condition. Discussing some of these issues,
Viveiros de Castro suggests that bad faith is the alternative to
anthropologists naïvely confusing 'taking seriously' with 'taking
literally' (2011: 135). Before this, he described (2004: 10) the
juggling necessary to the doing of anthropology as '*controlled
equivocation*' (§23). He has also discussed forms of perspectivism. Candea's response was that to take someone seriously does
not require sharing their beliefs, leaving open the possibility of
debate and discussion that Viveiros de Castro seems to fore-
close (2019). Making a similar point, Margery Wolf writes that
'in our desire to avoid objectifying our informants, we run the
risk of patronizing them' (1992: 135).

First Fernandez and Huber (2001) and then Michael Carrithers (2012) discussed this under the heading of irony. Carrithers describes anthropologists as having an ironic stance,
'one of detachment', in relation to the people they are studying.
However, this is not complete. For Carrithers, anthropologists
are, in the language of housing stock, semi-detached dwellings.
Our web of professional references and obligations relates not
only to the people we are with but also to our colleagues and,
through their work, to many other people worldwide. If we
subscribed only to one worldview, then we would necessarily
deny or contradict all other worldviews. The way to avoid such
dilemmas is not to fully play the game, perhaps by treating the
alternatives as *incommensurable* (§33) and refusing to judge be-

tween them. The result is that we are inevitably in a position of discomfort: we have ironicised our understanding by adopting a semi-detached stance that reflects our multiple (sometimes conflicting) allegiances.

Qv: *bifocal ethnography; equivocation; faithfulness; incommensurability*

References

Candea, M. 2019. *Comparison in Anthropology: The Impossible Method.* Cambridge: Cambridge University Press.

Carrithers, M. 2012. 'Seriousness, Irony and the Mission of Hyperbole', *Religion and Society* 3: 51–75.

Fernandez, J.W., and M.T. Huber. 2001. 'Introduction: The Anthropology of Irony', in J.W. Fernandez and M.T. Huber (eds), *Irony in Action: Anthropology, Practice and the Moral Imagination.* Chicago: University of Chicago Press, pp. 1–37.

Goffman, E. 1959. *The Presentation of Self in Everyday Life.* New York: Doubleday Anchor Books.

Just, R., and D. Zeitlyn. 2014. *Excursions in Realist Anthropology: A Merological Approach.* Newcastle upon Tyne: Cambridge Scholars Publishing.

Lewis, G. 1980. *Day of Shining Red: An Essay on Understanding ritual.* Cambridge: Cambridge University Press.

Nagel, T. 1980. The Limits of Objectivity. *Tanner Lectures 1979: Brasenose College, Oxford University.* Salt Lake City: Tanner Humanities Center.

Viveiros De Castro, E. 2004. 'Perspectival Anthropology and the Method of Controlled Equivocation', *Tipití: Journal of the Society for the Anthropology of Lowland South America* 2: 3–22.

———. 2011. 'Zeno and the Art of Anthropology', *Common Knowledge* 17: 128–45.

Wolf, M. 1992. *A Thrice Told Tale: Feminism, Postmodernism, & Ethnographic Responsibility.* Stanford: Stanford University Press.

37. Irrealism

The term irrealism was coined by the philosopher Nelson Goodman. Irrealism is the response by hard-nosed relativism to hard-nosed realism, but it becomes positively positivist in response to 'anything goes' relativism. Contentiously, irrealism succeeds when it irritates *both* positivists and relativists. In Goodman's words:

> Rather than argue over broad metaphysical issues, I am inclined to say 'Have it your own way; it matters not' (or, quoting from *Ways of Worldmaking*, 'Never mind mind, essence is not essential, and matter doesn't matter'). Let's look at the ways we work, the instruments we use, and the varied and fascinating results. At the beginning of the book realism and idealism, empiricism and rationalism, and many another doctrines are dismissed in favor of what I call irrealism, which is not one more doctrine – does not say that everything or anything is unreal – but is rather an attitude of unconcern with most issues between such doctrines. (1984: 43)

Goodman is being playful, but his point is valid: it might be more interesting, and more productive for anthropology as a discipline, to spend time thinking our way into ethnographies, rather than competing with philosophers on their theoretical turf. This amounts to an argument for an intellectual division of labour. The task of anthropology is to consider the ways in which humans live on earth, how people make sense (to themselves and to others) of their own lives and how external factors (other people and the world) impinge upon those lives. Of course, this inevitably impinges on the turf of philosophers, especially when we take a comparative tack and consider what sorts of generalisations about humans can be made across all the different case studies. The existence of overlap does not detract from the general observation that we start from different places. Be that as it may, Ian Hacking invokes irrealism as an alternative to the endlessly quarrelsome disputes between realisms and relativisms in the application of anthropological approaches to the study of experimentation as practised in laboratories.

References

Goodman, N. 1984. *Of Mind and Other Matters*. Harvard: Harvard University Press.
Hacking, I. 1988. 'The Participant Irrealist at Large in the Laboratory', *The British Journal for the Philosophy of Science* 39: 277–94.

38. Isolarion

James Atlee defines isolarion, in his book of this title, as 'the term for the fifteenth-century maps that describe specific areas in detail, but that do not provide a clarifying overview of how these places are related to each other'. Archaeological excavations of Roman mosaics provide another example of this phenomenon: some parts survive in an astonishingly good state of preservation, leaving a nose or an ear here, part of a bird there, but the whole mosaic may be frustratingly impossible to reconstruct. This issue often confronts anthropologists, who are frequently charged with not seeing the woods for the trees, or for failing to understand that the water is boiling despite (or because of) their concentration on the bubbles. One possible response to such charges is the method of specimens, which I discuss under *vignettes* (§59). Another response is the idea of *repleteness* (§49), which suggests that detail is useful for the discipline because it provides matter for reanalysis: what seems unnecessary or redundant detail to one may provide a significant hook for another, enabling a new reading unconsidered by the original researcher: so the discipline progresses. Other responses include pointing out that anthropologists, despite their obsession with details, are also very conscious of wider contexts, spatial and historical: one of the challenges of anthropology is the requirement to manage different scales of reference, to move nimbly between the minute and the large-scale. An alternative response is to accept the charge of tedious obsession but to highlight its benefits, not necessarily to the individual anthropologist but to

the collective whole: only by recording many similar cases can
we begin to appreciate overall patterns and to identify unusual
cases as being exceptions. For example, what may seem to be
'yet another study of nomadic pastoralism' might reveal highly
unusual gender relations and therefore be worth exploring differently from other studies of similar groups. Such comparisons would be impossible without the previous painstaking
collection of detail: the 'butterfly collecting' or 'stamp collecting', as it is often disparagingly dubbed. Like most academic
research, anthropology is a group endeavour, building on the
work of numerous researchers. We are collectively assembling
our own *mosaic* (§40), inking in details on a map that we know
will never be complete, since by the time we have finished one
part, others will be hopelessly out of date: research will never
be complete – we are always catching up. This is why the idea
of isolarion is useful, however much more research takes place!

Qv: *mosaics; repleteness; vignettes*

Reference

Attlee, J. 2007. *Isolarion: A Different Oxford Journey*. Chicago and London:
University of Chicago Press.

L

Life Writing

39. Life Writing

Every life is unique and as such is a *hapax* (§31). Every life story, no matter how unusual, illustrates the period and place in which it was set. These conflicting statements together explain why many researchers take a life history approach in their ethnographic research. Providing a *faithful* (§27) account of a life that is comprehensible to readers from widely disparate cultural traditions is far from easy. In effect, a life history becomes a peg on which a lot of ethnography can and should be hung. At the same time, the life story of an individual can pinpoint and illuminate specific factors that might be overlooked in the abstract generalisations of conventional ethnographic accounts of a society. Such illumination often arises from key life moments (discussed further in *epiphanies*, §20). Even without such moments, in order to make a life story comprehensible outside of its cultural tradition much ethnographic background must be given. *Prosopographies* (§48) typically provide the minimum of summary information, which is fleshed out by life histories.

Jerome Bruner (1984) distinguished between a life as lived, a life as experienced and a life as told. When we read or hear narratives about people's lives we are clearly dealing with lives as told, which have complicated relationships with lives as lived and lives as experienced. But who gets to create the narrative: the life subject or someone else? The question 'who does the telling?' points to the distinction between autobiography and biography. There are important differences between autoethnography, ethnographies at home and conventional ethnography by 'outsiders'. Sometimes these are about the extent to which the writer has made explicit the cultural background that is normally taken for granted between people with a shared upbringing. Despite all the advantages of autobiography, it can be hard for others to interpret, not only because background material may be taken for granted but also because of the (more or less deliberate) ways in which autobiographical accounts can mislead. Deborah Reed-Danahay considers the complexity and tensions in the introduction to her edited collection, discussing divergent uses of 'autoethnography' as referring to indigenous ethnography (in which the writer may not be central, discussed in the entry on *paraethnography*, §44), a form of autobiography drawing out the ethnographic implications or 'autobiographical ethnography' in which the anthropologist is in the frame as much as the culture being described. She settles on a definition of autoethnography as 'a form of self-narrative that places the self within a social context' (1997: 9).

The life stories that researchers write with and about their collaborators sometimes approach what might be called ghost-written autobiographies. Probably a better term for these is 'collaborative autobiographies', in which writer and subject together can address the complications posed by potential audiences that do not know the background and by the individual's version of events (Lejeune 1989: 265). Such texts are both complicated to produce and complex to analyse. While we need to recognise their complexity, we must also 'bracket off' this recognition (in ways that parallel the suspension of disbelief by a theatre audience) so that we too can participate in the 'autobiographical pact' (Lejeune's celebrated phrase) and take part in an autobiographical telling of a life.

When researching for a life history, it should not be assumed that all people can or want to talk about their lives in a single, coherent narrative. This form of account misleadingly suggests a narrative unity, based on the assumption that the adult I am now is the same person I was in my childhood and my youth. Work on Melanesian personhood and the idea of 'dividuals' (contrasting with individuals) deals with this issue, and similar concepts can be found in many cultural traditions. The researcher may 'create' the life story of a collaborator in more ways than one. When I decided to record the life story of Diko Madeleine, a senior woman who lived in Somié village in Cameroon, I found to my consternation that, after years of conversations with Diko and her children, I had collected only a mass of historical fragments that did not add up to a whole life story. Wondering how to produce from these shreds an account that was faithful to her life, I eventually described the process as creating an anthropological silhouette rather than a complete portrait. Narrative fragments can contribute to an overall *mosaic* (§40) if they are bolstered by complementary (triangulating) research of many different types focused on the same place, region or person.

Work on the social life of *things* (§56) has led to the development of what Kopytoff calls their 'social biographies'. These apply life history approaches to things, and in some cases can include *epiphanic moments* (§20): consider the shift in the lives of Phidias' sculptures when they were moved from Athens to London in the early nineteenth century!

Qv: *epiphanies*; *faithfulness*; *hapax*; *prosopography*

References

Bruner, E.M. 1984. 'Introduction: The Opening Up of Anthropology', in E.M. Bruner (ed.), *Text, Play, and Story: The Construction and Reconstruction of Self and Society*. Washington, D.C.: American Ethnological Society, pp. 1–16.

Kopytoff, I. 1986. 'The Cultural Biography of Things: Commoditization as Process', in A. Appadurai (ed.), *The Social Life of Things: Commodities in Cultural Perspective*. Cambridge: Cambridge University Press, pp. 64–94.

Lejeune, P. 1989. *On Autobiography*. Minneapolis: University of Minnesota Press.

Reed-Danahay, D.E. 1997. 'Introduction', in D.E. Reed-Danahay (ed.), *Auto/ethnography: Rewriting the Self and the Social*. Oxford: Berg, pp. 1–17.

Zeitlyn, D. 2008. 'Life History Writing and the Anthropological Silhouette', *Social Anthropology* 16(2): 154–71.

M

Mosaics

Meaning: see *Commitment*

Meaning Finitism: see *Finitism*

Montage: see *Collage*

40. Mosaics

Thinking about mosaics invites us to think about compositional strategies and hybridity. It invites us to think about these things as features of the world, affecting how people make societies and live their lives, as well as how they feature in accounts by social scientists of different social groups. For the first strand, Ann Brouwer Stahl talks about:

> the mosaic quality of African social, political economic, and technological landscapes, mosaics in which foragers interacted with agriculturalists, peripatetic herders passed through the courts of kings, and so-called tribal societies formed on the margins of complex polities. (2004: 147)

Stahl uses the idea of mosaics as a way of exploring the complexity of African political and economic systems. She does not much discuss the metaphor she has chosen. Mosaics are the original tessellated surfaces; the constituent tiles catch the light at various angles; they glitter while they represent. They are made from a variety of materials to produce a palette of colours and tones. (Concerns about symmetry and Penrose tiling are unfortunately too far off topic here.) Stahl says:

> Guyer and Belinga posit compositional strategies of leadership that brought together people with diverse, complexly organized knowledges (of crafts, the supernatural, diverse ecologies, and economic opportunities). Compositional strategies resonate with notions of heterarchy and are 'quite different from the models of hierarchical gradations of esoteric knowledge as a social control mechanism'. (2004: 148)

Stahl is right: Guyer and Belinga's idea of 'compositional strategies' is very close to her use of mosaics. The picture is composite, the result of happenstance and bricolage *not* following from a discrete or finite set of central principles or structures. Guyer and Belinga argue for a correction of the African stereotype that the primary source of wealth is wealth-in-people. They suggest that, in the central African forest zone, there was also a knowledge economy. The clearest examples concern knowledge of smelting technologies. The ability to make a metal from 'rock' is profoundly unusual, and/or scary, and is therefore power-giving. Knowledge is fragmentary and arguable, but it is as important as people. As Guyer and Belinga say, 'only those who know can act and not everyone knows the same things' (1995: 102). On their account, 'Society is not integrated; it is a constant improvisation along a continuum from centrifugality to brilliant synergism' (1995: 103). They argue for a compositional approach in which knowledge is splintered, and putting things together conceptually is as valuable as doing the same materially.

This is little different from Amselle's assault on the fixity of ethnic identity (1998). Although I think he overstates his case, in an overly postmodern presentation of the fluidity of ethnic identity, it is a valuable corrective that forces us to think more about how the supposed fixity of ethnic identity should be seen, not as a pre-existing given but as an achievement, a cultural creation. For Amselle, a culture is an agreement about what we can argue about (and therefore an example of an *essentially contested concept*, §24). It is a meta-agreement, acting as a form of *boundary object* (§10). No agreement is needed about what our heritage is, but the recognition that we have or should have a heritage gives us common ground from which to argue these matters out. On Amselle's account of the Mande area, part of the reason why Wahabist Islam has spread there is that so many Moslems are recent converts and so, to distinguish themselves from others (e.g. their neighbours), some insist that they are part of a global movement *without* local correlates: a form of Islamic fundamentalism. In order to understand local complexities, you need a wider than local perspective. This may be a useful corrective to help understanding Mande and regional factors (covering the intersections of present-day Mali, Senegal and Burkina Faso). Moreover, it returns us to Malinowski's early argument from 'Argonauts of the Western Pacific' that cultures are not isolated entities. To my mind, Amselle also evokes Leach's discussion of Kachin in Highland Burma as a *dynamic* system (or clash of systems), so perhaps the approach is not as new as it may seem. However, the major weakness in Amselle's thesis is the insistence that people have a radical freedom to act. This ignores the systematicity of constraints that mutual expectations place on individual freedom. For example, if you cannot speak Fulfulde and are not Moslem, you could say 'I am Fulani', but it would be ridiculous. Literally you would be ridiculed and never accepted. There *are* patterns that can be described (perhaps as *figurations*, §28). Otherwise, social life would be unliveable: some consistency and predictability are necessary (although perhaps less than one might think).

I hope this illustrates some of the dilemmas involved when practising anthropology (and social science more generally). The task is to preserve babies while draining the bathwater. In terms of the metaphor of mosaics, while Amselle stresses the freedom to choose any individual tile in a mosaic, I think he loses sight of the constraints imposed by the overall design. An individual may be able to choose between some tiles, but not all tiles are available or appropriate for a particular position.

How well does the concept of mosaics characterise the results of social science? This book is itself an argument for the dappled anthropology proposed by Nancy Cartwright (see the Introduction above). Cartwright not only argues for a 'dappled world' described in a patchwork fashion; she also encourages us to develop 'methodologies for life in the messy world which we invariably inhabit' (1999: 18). This connects intimately with the two aspects of mosaics that I have been discussing.

Qv: *isolarion; vignettes*

References

Amselle, J.-L. 1998. *Mestizo Logics: Anthropology of Identity in Africa and Elsewhere*. Stanford, CA: Stanford University Press.

Cartwright, N. 1999. *The Dappled World: A Study of the Boundaries of Science*. Cambridge: Cambridge University Press.

Guyer, J.I. and S.M.E. Belinga. 1995. 'Wealth in People as Wealth in Knowledge: Accumulation and Composition in Equatorial Africa', *Journal of African History* 36: 91–120.

Leach, E.R. 1954. *The Political Systems of Highland Burma*. London: Athlone Press.

Malinowski, B. 1922. *Argonauts of the Western Pacific*. London: Routledge & Kegan Paul.

Stahl, A.B. 2004. 'Political Economic Mosaics: Archaeology of the Last Two Millennia in Tropical Sub-Saharan Africa', *Annual Review of Anthropology* 33: 145–72.

N

Non-ergodicity

41. Non-ergodicity

All the elements of an ergodic system are identical (think of billiard balls, and the role of atoms in classical physics). In a non-ergodic system, that rule does not hold: imagine how physics would be if each atom had unique properties. Curiously, in the social sciences and humanities this concept is usually referred to in its negative form: much more is written about non-ergodic than ergodic systems. Tolstoy's novel *Anna Karenina* opens with the famous generalisation 'All happy families resemble each other; each unhappy family is unhappy in its own way' (1873). In the language of sociology, Tolstoy is saying that happy families are ergodic, but unhappy families are non-ergodic: they are unique unto themselves. Whether or not we dispute Tolstoy's generalisation, the difference is clear. In a non-ergodic system, we cannot assume that all parts behave or develop in the same way, so it is not possible to generalise from the study of a small part of that system. This sounds like conventional criticism of anthropology by sociologists, economists or even medical scientists. However, anthropologists do not use their case studies to make large-scale or global predictions in the same way as other disciplines, and the methods of such critics do not enable them to make generalisations in non-ergodic systems, as they might suggest. Hence the continual surprise at events in the world. Be that as it may, recognising that we are dealing with non-ergodic systems helps to guard against unthinking social determinism. *Prosopographical* (§48) approaches and *life history* (§39) enable us to recognise the common features of non-ergodic events.

Qv: *hapax*; *equifinality*; *prosopography*; *vignettes*

Non-representation: see **Representation**

O

Ostension

Ontography: see *Epistemography*

42. Ostension

Ostension, showing things, plays an important role in discussions of representation and meaning. Ostension has been
positioned as an alternative to representation: rather than representing something, I merely show it, in the hope that viewers
can see what I am talking about. A definition by *exemplar* (§26)
is often an instance of ostension: 'if you want to know what
a dog is then I will show you one' (or better, 'I will show you
several'). By showing exemplars rather than unusual instances
or outliers, I can convey an idea of the typical case, the 'nor-
mal', without any reference to essences or essential properties.
In practice, this seems to work within communities, but it may
be less reliable for the purposes of radical translation. Quine's
thought experiment leaves learners uncertain: they are in an
aporia (§3) about whether they have been shown 'rabbits' or
'rabbit-parts'. I suspect this is a needlessly artificial consequence
of the thought experiment: by the time a language learner has
been permitted to accompany a hunter and been shown small
animals, they will probably have sufficient language skills to enable a conversation about the process, so connecting the term in
question to many others, and to the semantic network in which
it occurs, and addressing the problems of *finitism* (§29). This
would not satisfy a philosopher determined to hold Quine's po-

sition, but it may work for a pragmatic anthropologist prepared to accept, and bracket off, that lingering possibility of mistake and confusion.

Another way to think about potential problems with ostension in contexts of cross-cultural interaction is to recognise the potential cultural inflection of ostension (recognising that acts of ostension are culture-laden). A hinterland of more or less expert knowledge is invoked or tacitly assumed so that the learner can see what they are shown. Judith Okely described this nicely (2001) in a case study that uses the effects of expert knowledge to demonstrate that perception is active. In her example, a farmer and a non-farmer look through a window at a field of cows, and the farmer understands the view in ways that the non-farmer does not: while the latter merely *looks*, the farmer *sees* the potential agricultural problems in the same field. This leaves anthropologists with the conundrum of how to acquire the expert knowledge to enable them to see as the farmer sees. The way I understand this mitigates the dilemma. Knowledge is not an either/or attribute such that one has either all or none of the expert knowledge in question. Rather, it's a matter of degree; one can gather knowledge incrementally: in the terms of Okely's contrast, slowly coming to *see*. Comprehension can improve with time, allowing earlier misapprehensions to be corrected. By implication, the claims we make must be modest, which is another argument for humility and partiality (incompleteness). It is an argument for a sparse anthropology.

Another loosely connected usage of the term ostension is explored by the folklorists Linda Dégh and Andrew Vázsonyi, who appropriated it in their 1983 article 'Does the Word "Dog" Bite?' to refer to ways in which real-life actions are influenced by legends (whether knowingly or not). There are sadly (a few) instances of legends being acted out in real life, including copycat murders and poisoned sweets being given out at Halloween. Perhaps more relevant to anthropologists is the application of these ideas to ritual performance. For example, a healing ritual may be held to achieve health by enacting it. For Dégh and Vázsonyi this would be a case of ostension.

Qv: *agnosia; aporia; exemplar; finitism; Hesse nets; translation*

References

Dégh, L., and A. Vázsonyi. 1983. 'Does the Word "Dog" Bite? Ostensive Action: A Means of Legend-Telling', *Journal of Folklore Research* 20: 5–34.

Grasseni, C. 2007. 'Communities of Practice and Forms of Life: Towards a Rehabilitation of Vision?', in M. Harris (ed.), *Ways of Knowing: Anthropological Approaches to Crafting Experience and Knowledge*. Oxford: Berghahn, pp. 203–21.

Okely, J. 2001. 'Visualism and Landscape: Looking and Seeing in Normandy', *Ethnos* 66: 99–120.

P

Palimpsest Memory; Paraethnography; Partial Views and Partiality; Pattern Language; Positioning Theory; Prosopography

43. Palimpsest Memory

Palimpsest is a lovely word, and I am pleased to include it here, where it merits inclusion because of the way it evokes the over-lapping and layering of fragments of incomplete information. As such, it is a good metaphor for anthropological research. The idea of palimpsest comes from textual scholarship and refers to old parchment documents on which some writing has been erased and overwritten, sometimes eventually re-emerging. The resulting text is a palimpsest: a mixture of original and revised words written at different times. Applying the idea to mem-ory raises two issues. The first and less controversial suggestion is that when considering cultural heritage we are dealing with palimpsest memories, involving accreted layers of recollection. Labelling something as heritage adds a different layer or fram-ing to a memory, so the memory cannot simply be taken as referring directly to its source.

Aleida Assman discusses something similar when consider-ing the distinction between 'canon' and 'archive': the very de-cision that an object is worthy of preservation in a museum or archive changes the way in which that object is perceived and understood. As contributors to De Jong and Rowlands' ed-ited collection make clear, a similar process can occur when a dance or a piece of material culture is identified as constituting heritage (2007). Anyone considering it thereafter will have to contend with the heritage framing and consider the ways in which the parts of the palimpsest interact and possibly obscure each other.

A more controversial suggestion is that all memory is a form of palimpsest, since remembering is always an active re-creation in the present. This has been demonstrated, for example, by exploring how people present in New York in September 2001 remembered seeing the aeroplanes hitting the twin towers (so-called flashbulb memories, which, it turns out, can change over time (Hirst et al. 2015)). Maurice Bloch discusses a less dramatic instance of how individuals in Madagascar talk about a battle in which their grandparents may have fought, but by talking in the first person they elide the generations, making a palimpsest of personal identities and of memories of the event.

References

Assmann, A. 2008. 'Canon and Archive', in A. Erll, A. Nünning and S.B. Young (eds), *Cultural Memory Studies: An International and Interdisciplinary Handbook*. Berlin: Walter de Gruyter, pp. 97–107.

Bloch, M. 1998. 'Autobiographical Memory and the Historical Memory of the More Distant Past', in *How We Think They Think: Anthropological Approaches to Cognition, Memory, and Literacy*. Boulder Colorado: Westview Press, pp. 114–27.

De Jong, F., and M.J. Rowlands. 2007. 'Reconsidering Heritage and Memory in Africa: Introduction', in F. De Jong and M.J. Rowlands (eds), *Reclaiming Heritage: Alternative Imaginaries of Memory in West Africa*. Walnut Creek, CA: Left Coast Press, pp. 1–30.

Hirst, W. et al. 2015. 'A Ten-Year Follow-Up of a Study of Memory for the Attack of September 11, 2001: Flashbulb Memories and Memories for Flashbulb Events', *Journal of Experimental Psychology: General* 144: 604–23.

Paraconsistency: see *Dialetheism*

44. Paraethnography

The way in which a society or social group understands itself could, by analogy with terms such as ethnobotany and ethnozoology, be called 'ethnoethnograpy': however, the accepted term of art is paraethnography. As coined by Douglas Holmes and George Marcus, this originally described the way in which local experts undertake analysis that is ethnographic, such that they should be treated as colleagues rather than as research subjects. Douglas Holmes worked with senior bankers during his research on international banking. He set out to get them talking and then summarise how they understood the system. I want to generalise their position and the use of the term. As I see it, all human actors have anthropological understandings of the world they live in – that is what enables social interaction! Researchers merely tease out that understanding, make it explicit and write it down. To be a competent social actor, a person must gain some fluency in one or more dialects of one or more languages. In so doing they acquire not only a linguistic grammar but also a social grammar, which determines how words should be used and in which contexts they should be avoided. They must also learn how to comport themselves, how to hold their body, which bits of it to display, when and to whom. They must learn which parts can be surgically altered (through the insertion of metal, plastic, silicon or ink) and to whom they should admit having had such procedures. The list could be continued. The models of understanding that people have of their fellow actors are essentially anthropological understandings, despite being unformalised, unstated and rarely comparative. Since this works on the street, why not in academe? Our understanding of our fellow citizens is imperfect, incomplete *and* biased to our points of view (see *partiality*, §45), but it more or less works. It is adequate for our everyday lives, and in achieving that adequacy it has passed a kind of test, repeatedly. The challenge for twenty-first century anthropology is to abandon the requirements of completeness and certainty in favour of what I call sparse anthropology. We should keep trying to make explicit the complexity and systematicity, the inconsistency, clarity and *vagueness* (§58) of everyday understandings. Different participants may provide very different paraethnographies to which we try to remain *faithful* (§27). Our accounts may synthesise many paraethnographies, but the idea reminds us that the accounts produced are not our impositions. Ethnographies aspire to report 'their' understandings not 'ours', even if the best we can report is 'our understandings of their understandings'.

Qv: *faithfulness*; *partiality*

References

Holmes, D., and G. Marcus. 2005. 'Cultures of Expertise and the Management of Globalisation: Towards the Re-Functioning of Ethnography', in A. Ong and S.J. Collier (eds), *Global Assemblages: Technology, Politics, and Ethics as Anthropological Problems*. Oxford: Blackwell, pp. 235–52.

Holmes, D.R. 2009. 'Economy of Words', *Cultural Anthropology* 24: 381–419.

45. Partial Views and Partiality

The word *partial* in English means both (1) incomplete and (2) biased. Both meanings are relevant to anthropology. Anthropological accounts are inevitably incomplete and biased and should be explicitly recognised as such. Only by recognising these limitations can we try to reduce them. Recognising that partiality cannot be eradicated does not absolve us from trying to minimise it. The inevitability of bias does not prevent an anthropologist from seeking to document its occurrence. This applies equally to our own and our informants' partiality. Standard sociological research techniques remain helpful, providing warrants for our statements. On the basis of these methods, anthropologists are systematic. They do not believe everything they are told: they listen to what everyone tells them and then try to make sense of the contradictions between what different people say and between what someone says and what they do. This often puts anthropologists in a position of *ironic detachment* (§36).

Accepting that we do not and cannot know everything requires humility. It is also a necessary consequence of a scientific orientation: as Hastrup puts it, 'knowledge must be *organized* information; in the case of anthropology it concerns the organized information about ways of living in the world and modes of attending to the world. The organization implies that knowledge is both *reductive* and *selective*' (2004: 456, original emphases).

Incompleteness leaves room for multiple other accounts, and acknowledging it is a necessary part of anthropology's abstention from claims of exclusivity, of privileged access to truth. Claims to exclusivity create a demarcated domain whose boundaries are continually being challenged and shown to have been misunderstood. We should explicitly acknowledge our own partialities; depending on the rhetoric used, such recognition could be described as either scientific or postmodern. An honest awareness that our accounts are both incomplete and biased produces a more knowing anthropological understanding that is clearer for its admission of incompleteness.

Qv: *paraethnography*, *vagueness*

References

Hastrup, K. 2004. 'Getting it Right: Knowledge and Evidence in Anthropology', *Anthropological Theory* 4: 455–72.

Zeitlyn, D. 2009. 'Understanding Anthropological Understanding: For a Merological Anthropology', *Anthropological Theory* 9(2): 209–31.

46. Pattern Language

This architectural idea is a promising way of thinking about ritual and history. The architect Christopher Alexander describes pattern language thus: 'each pattern describes a problem which occurs over and over again in our environment, and then describes the core of the solution to that problem, in such a way that you can use this solution a million times over, without ever doing it the same way twice'. The idea is that we find not repetition in a strict sense but variations on a theme, the themes being the patterns.

The idea of a pattern language is summed up in the saying 'history does not repeat itself, but it rhymes'. This is conventionally attributed to Mark Twain, but without much foundation. Twain actually said: 'History never repeats itself, but the Kaleidoscopic combinations of the pictured present often seem to be constructed out of the broken fragments of antique legends' (Twain and Warner 1972: 430). The actual quotation and the apocryphal one can be seen as variants of each other, and as such are instances of a pattern language.

Martin et al. (2001) apply the idea of pattern languages in ethnographic research to how people use computer systems, drawing out patterns in repeated instances of people's interactions with computers, grouping them as instances of the same 'sort of thing', which makes this a type of *colligation* (§15). More generally, the idea is implicit in Mauss's rites of passage, a structure common to many disparate rituals. It is also implicit in the idea of *chronotopes* (§13) (which identify common themes or patterns in how people conceptualise time). Thinking about pattern languages encourages us to expect similarity and resemblance, rather than identical repetitions of events, be they ritual performances or everyday work tasks. Each event has been performed before, perhaps by the same people, but each time the details are different. The challenge for ethnographic approaches (as for the performers) is to identify the sort of event that is being attempted, the details that make it of this particular type, and why other details are irrelevant to its identification as 'that sort of thing'.

Qv: *colligation*

References

Alexander, C. 1979. *The Timeless Way of Building*. New York: Oxford University Press.

Alexander, C., S. Ishikawa and M. Silverstein. 1977. *A Pattern Language: Towns, Buildings, Construction*. New York: Oxford University Press.

Martin, D., et al. (eds). Proceedings of the seventh European Conference on Computer Supported Cooperative Work (ECSCW), 16–20 September 2001, Bonn, Germany. Dordrecht: Kluwer Academic Publishers, pp. 39–58.

Twain, M., and C.D. Warner. 1972. *The Gilded Age: A Tale of To-Day*. Indianapolis: Bobbs-Merrill.

Perspective: see *Axonometric Projection*

47. Positioning Theory

Positioning theory was developed in social psychology as an alternative to frames or roles. More dynamic than these alternatives, it seeks to bring semantics and morality back into social psychology. Positioning theory places key importance on the cultural context of events, and therefore presents a way in which anthropology and psychology can resume former partnerships and dialogue. These seem to have diminished over recent years, challenged by suspicions of positivism on one hand and an emphasis on laboratory experimentation on the other. Positioning theory provides a framework for discussing dynamic events and

how individuals reflexively and knowingly play their parts in
them as the events evolve. To do this, Harré et al. say that participants must have available 'a repertoire of narrative conventions'
(2009: 10). They mean more than merely verbal conventions, social roles as identified by *figuration* (§28) or *colligation* (§15), but
they are excluding the larger-scale, explicitly defined social roles.
By contrast, the positions taken or struck, the stances adopted
during an interaction, are on a smaller scale and often fleeting. As
such, positioning theory is concerned with microdynamics rather
than being a wholesale redescription of social anthropology for
psychology. It contains important ideas for social scientists about
the importance of attending to the dynamic and changing ways
in which individuals respond to particular circumstances, granted
a larger social context. Some of the cases discussed by Harré et
al. (2009) show how it can be used in practice to analyse shifting
and conflicting attributions of positions between participants in
social dramas. Positioning theory has a parallel in *argumentation
theory* (§5) in that the former is to people what the latter is to
concepts. Both rely on forms of *colligation* (§15) and *figuration*
(§28) to identify elements or positions that are in flux: here, the
positions people adopt, however fleetingly.

Qv: *argumentation theory; commitment; figuration*

References

Davies, B., and R. Harré. 1990. 'Positioning: The Discursive Production of
    Selves', *Journal for the Theory of Social Behaviour* 20: 43–63.
Harré, R., et al. 2009. 'Recent Advances in Positioning Theory', *Theory & Psy-
    chology* 19: 5–31.

Projection: see *Axonometric Projection*

48. Prosopography

Prosopography is the study of individuals. The term comes from classics and was originally a list of all the people known to have lived in Classical Rome: an archaeological compilation of inscriptions on funerary monuments. The Church of Latter-day Saints' project to collate birth and death registers and thus compile a genealogy of the entire human population (with the goal of retrospectively baptising them into the church) is a form of prosopography. In some ways, so too are most types of *life writing* (§39). Prosopography celebrates uniqueness and accepts that our knowledge of people is often shockingly incomplete. Because individuals are unique, each prosopography is a *hapax* (§31). In many cases of classical prosopography, all we have is a name, sometimes not even complete. Entries may be as slender as 'Someone called Huomnuar lived at about this time and died in this place'. Anthropology can do better than classical studies here because we are blessed with direct access to the 'source material'. This enables us to write substantially more detailed prosopographical records of those with whom we work.

Prosopography started with a relentless focus on individuals. It is now used to talk about populations, and about subgroups within a population. In history, this often concerns the genealogical and economic interconnections among elites, but the concept of prosopography also provides a framework for discussing the broader social contexts of groups of people, where little may be known about the individuals. In different disciplines, this may be called collective biography or career-line analysis. Another way of seeing this is as the extraction of ergodic principles from the *non-ergodic* (§41) individual members of a group. (In an ergodic population, any single individual is representative of the entire population, which is often not true of non-ergodic humans.) Some prosopographical approaches have been taken up by what is now called social network analysis (itself an anthropological innovation from the 1960s) without realising the kinship to earlier work in the same field. Perhaps this lack of recognition was because early prosopography did not use the same mathematical tools, let alone visualisation techniques such as social network analysis. Happily, this has changed, and prosopography's apparently obsessive collection of minutely detailed information about individuals can be used to justify generalisations about groups: substance for both sociology and history.

Qv: *hapax*; *isolarion*; *life writing*; *non-ergodicity*

Reference

Stone, L. 1987. 'Prosopography', *The Past and the Present Revisited* (Revised edition). London: Routledge & Kegan Paul, pp. 45–73.

R

Repleteness; Representation/Non-representation; Representational Force

49. Repleteness

Nelson Goodman uses *repleteness* in discussing the semantic density of pictorial and other representations. It is a nice alternative to Gilbert Ryle's idea of thick description (imported into anthropology by Clifford Geertz). Goodman starts by contrasting calibrated and uncalibrated thermometers (note for younger readers: old thermometers were a thin tube containing mercury, which expanded with heat). Both show temperature changes, but the calibrated one has greater semantic density. Repleteness enters with the reflection that the only thing that matters is the height of the mercury column: other features of thermometers (e.g. the thickness of the tube) are irrelevant, and if one concentrates on those aspects then perhaps the 'idea' of a thermometer has not been grasped. Similarly with graphs, I could show two identical images: of a graph charting stock price movements (to use Goodman's example) and a sketch of distant mountains. In the first, it would be a misunderstanding of what the image conveys to concentrate on the thickness of the line and its qualities. In the second, it would be a misunderstanding of what a sketch is *not* to do so. For Goodman, there are degrees of repleteness, and graphs are minimally replete. This approach is applicable to anthropological accounts: we can think about the semantic density (or repleteness) of an ethnography. The more replete the ethnographic account, the easier it is to reanalyse, and to draw conclusions about the material that differ from those of the author.

Qv: *representational force*

References

Goodman, N. 1976. *Languages of Art: An Approach to a Theory of Symbols.* Indianapolis: Hackett publishing.

———. 1984. *Of Mind and Other Matters.* Harvard: Harvard University Press.

Ryle, G. 1971. 'The Thinking of Thoughts: What is "le Penseur" Doing?', *Collected papers. Volume 2.* London: Hutchinson, pp. 480–96.

50. Representation/Non-representation

Representation has come in for a lot of criticism. Some of this is justified, but it has been overdone. Spivak seized on a key ambiguity in the idea of representation, which means both Darstellung, 'proxy and portrait', and Vertretung, 'speaking for'. She viewed the former as good and the latter as bad (see Devadas and Nicholls 2002: 82–83). This makes talk of representation uncomfortable for many, but I think the discomfort is positive. We should continue to use the term but with cautious awareness of the attendant pitfalls. I do not think it is possible to avoid representation (*pace* Nigel Thrift). Nor do I think it possible to change the human condition. Consequently, we must accept that power plays and representative plays (plays on representation) are inescapable. Academic researchers are not the only people to represent social groups: it is a common human practice. We need a terminology for discussing social groups (meta-anthropology): a way of talking about how people talk about social groups. However fraught it may be, we need a term like representation. I considered alternatives such as 'characterisation', but in the end (although not without trepidation) I returned to representation as the best option.

Johannes Fabian criticises what he calls 'representationism': 'The aim is to assign to representing a more modest, less imperial, place in a theory of knowledge, not to exorcise by decree what is obviously an important human capacity' (1990: 756). This seems to be what Nigel Thrift has in mind in his non-representational programme. Thrift stresses embodied experience and ongoing process/ praxis, not the end results of process. It is an argument for the recognition of politics and a reminder that there are no non-political positions. Despite all, we still end up with (hopefully modest and *partial*, §45) representations.

In a different but related field, Eelco Runia discusses photographic representation. Runia stresses *presence* as opposed to representation (2006). On his account, images are experientially present: forms of haunting, perhaps. This raises, in a good way, some old issues about what being 'experientially present' actually means.

Qv: *commitment*

References

Devadas, V., and B. Nicholls. 2002. 'Postcolonial Interventions: Gayatri Spivak, Three Wise Men and the Native Informant', *Critical Horizons* 3: 73–101.

Fabian, J. 1990. 'Presence and Representation: The Other and Anthropological Writing', *Critical Inquiry* 16: 753–72.

Runia, E. 2006. 'Presence', *History and Theory* 45: 1–29.

Spivak, G.C. 1988. 'Can the Subaltern Speak?', in C. Nelson and L. Grossberg (eds), *Marxism and Interpretation of Culture*. Urbana and Chicago: University of Illinois Press, pp. 271–313.

Thrift, N.J. 2007. *Non-Representational Theory: Space, Politics, Affect*. London and New York: Routledge.

51. Representational Force

Two novelty postcards demonstrate the point: *Brighton at Night* and *Brighton in the Fog*. It is not necessary to show them to convey the idea: one is entirely black, the other uniformly dull grey. What makes them postcards of Brighton? Nothing but the caption. Cynics such as me might doubt that anyone actually stood on the Brighton seafront with a camera to take either image, but, on a more serious point, they could have done and indeed *should* have done. What is a word like 'should' doing here? It marks the establishment of what can be termed the 'representing relationship'. Without it, representation fails (as with the fictional postcards), which is why 'should' is there. The word *force* evokes John Austin's speech acts, but this case concerns representational acts. The parallel suggests that we ask how something is made into a representation. Representational force captures the act of baptism, the establishment of the deictic link between name and named, between image and its subject (the thing portrayed), and between the concept and the thing conceived (perhaps through *ostension*, §42). Representational force is liminal: it stands between the representation per se and the object represented; it is the glue that enables representation to work by sticking those pieces together. Against this, versions of direct realism deny the need for a linking entity. Or we could wonder whether it might be enough simply to say 'this *is* a representation' (a form of naïve representation). I would say no: tempting though it may be, that approach just will not work; the connections need to be spelled out because so many different types of representation are possible (as illustrated by the discussion of *axonometric projections*, §7). As Spivak made clear, representations have politics, even those that aspire to neutrality and deny that they are political. They are created for a purpose. Recognising their biases and their *partiality* (§45) or incompleteness is the first step towards continuing with representations knowingly and recognising the dangers inherent in them.

Qv: *ostension*; *representation*

References

Austin, J.L. 1962. *How to Do Things with Words*. Oxford: Clarendon Press.
Spivak, G.C. 1988. 'Can the Subaltern Speak?', in C. Nelson and L. Grossberg (eds), *Marxism and Interpretation of Culture*. Urbana and Chicago: University of Illinois Press, pp. 271–313.

S

Sgraffiti; Stochastic Variation; Synaesthesia

Semi-propositional Representations: see *Boundary Objects*

52. Sgraffiti

There is a set of words relating to ideas of incomplete, partial evidence for aspects of human activity. All of these words can be applied to material used in research in ways unintended and often unimaginable by their creators ('witnesses in spite of themselves'). Such materials include records or objects that at the time were inconsequential but that can later be made to tell a wider and more significant story. The three key terms are sgraffiti, scars or scarification and vestiges, all of which are forms of traces (Hauser 2007: 102–3).

Sgraffito derives from the Italian *graffiare*, 'to scratch'. In pottery, it denotes a decorative technique in which multiple layers of slip or glaze are applied to a pot, then layers are scratched off to reveal underlying colours. More generally, the term is used of *palimpsests* (§43) and other layered composites, in which earlier forms re-emerge through superimposed layers. Scarring is more dramatic and violent and usually unplanned or unintended. Like sgraffiti, scars are tangible reminders of the processes of their creation. A scar evokes the event (wounding) that produced it (Rugg 1997: 238). Scars are a kind of vestige, something that remains after the 'main event' has passed. All these traces can become evidence (similarly, *archaeologists* (§4) use rubbish to support narratives about the people who discarded it).

Discussing *life writing* (§39), Smith and Watson (2001: 130) cite a similar metaphor used by Michel Leiris, which partially defined him; he talked of autobiography as 'scratching' out a set of marks.

Qv: *life writing, palimpsests*

References

Hauser, K. 2007. *Shadow Sites: Photography, Archaeology, and the British Landscape 1927–1955*. Oxford: Oxford University Press.
Rugg, L.H. 1997. *Picturing Ourselves: Photography & Autobiography*. Chicago: University of Chicago Press.
Smith, S., and J. Watson 2001. 'The Rumpled Bed of Autobiography: Extravagant Lives, Extravagant Questions'. *Biography* 24: 1–14.

53. Stochastic Variation

This idea helps us think about the meaning of randomness. Stochastic variation is random variation around a goal. Since the definition involves a target, stochastic variables are not completely random, and the term should not be used as a synonym for randomness in general. The idea captures something of the play of everyday life, the tugs that emerge from the give and take of life as lived, as opposed to the simplifying conceptual structures we use to think about it. Every scientific experiment is imperfect, every ritual could have been better performed, every meal better cooked. Yet idealised versions are given in scientific papers, theological texts and recipe books. Stochastic variation helps us clarify the ideals, the goals being aspired to, and to identify these amongst the complexities of real-life instances. People (and researchers) use *figuration* (§28) to identify goals despite the randomness surrounding them.

Qv: *figuration*

Surprise: see *Epiphanies*

54. Synaesthesia

Synaesthesia is the experience of simultaneously combined senses. Examples include sounds perceived as colours, touch experienced as scent and so on. It is commonly associated with psychedelic drugs and other forms of heightened or altered consciousness. Those who experience synaesthesia experience it only some of the time; most people, however, never do. Some people find it enriches their lives; others experience synaesthesia as a disorienting and distracting clinical condition that they wish to be free of. Regardless of this, it is important to understand that an instance of synaesthesia involves only one experience: not separate experiences of sound and colour, but it is a single experience whose description requires a fusion of the ways in which we usually talk about sound and colour. Those who have not experienced synaesthesia struggle to understand what it feels like, and those who have experienced it find it hard to convey. As such, it becomes a metaphoric touchstone for the difficulty (some would say impossibility) of ethnographic research. The entries on *translation* (§57), *equivocation* (§23) and *partial* (incomplete) accounts (§45) touch on the same issue in different ways. Perhaps we must reconcile ourselves to the fact that in writing ethnographic accounts we are at best moving from synaesthetic experience to its use as a metaphor. This is inevitable as we move across media, creating *ekphrases* (§18) that bridge languages and forms of experience. Diana Young discusses the connections made by Australian Western Desert people (Anangu, Pitjantjatjara and Yankunytjatjara) between colours and smells. She argues that this is culturally constructed and part of a wider pattern connecting people (healthy people) and the land, especially the land after rain. She includes haptics and 'ways of being in the land' with the way that important plants such as wild tobacco 'smell of green'. She concludes that such socially learned synaesthetic experiences may constitute 'a different way of thinking' (2005: 73).

Qv: *ekphrasis*; *equivocation*; *translation*; *partiality*

Reference

Young, D. 2005. 'The Smell of Greenness: Cultural Synaesthesia in the Western Desert', *Etnofoor* 18: 61–77.

T

Teleoanalysis; Things; Translation (Anthropological Translation)

55. Teleoanalysis

Teleoanalysis can be defined as the synthesis of different categories of evidence to obtain a quantitative general summary of (a) the relation between a cause of a disease and the risk of the disease and (b) the extent to which the disease can be prevented. Teleoanalysis is different from meta-analysis because it relies on combining data from different classes of evidence rather than one type of study.
— N.J. Wald and J.K. Morris, 'Teleoanalysis'

For all its explicitly quantitative origin, as made clear in Wald and Morris's definition, this is a useful term for (methodological) triangulation. Triangulation comes from early navigation methods using compasses and paper maps. Teleoanalysis is not navigationally inspired so does not invoke a geographical or spatial substratum. It describes ways of combining various research materials collected using different sources, each with different strengths and weaknesses. As with *cables* (§11), the strength of the ensemble is not limited by that of the weakest component. Generalising to include qualitative approaches, teleoanalysis concerns the synthesis of disparate materials and types of data, enabling the identification of causal patterns of connection. That concern with causation makes it a form of *colligation* (§15), but teleoanalysis emphasises the diversity of sources and the ways in which they can be combined.

Q̲v̲: *cabling, colligation*

Reference

Wald, N.J., and J.K. Morris. 2003. 'Teleoanalysis: Combining Data from Different Types of Study', *BMJ* 327: 616–18.

Tesserae: **see** *Mosaics*

56. Things

In 2001, Bill Brown asked why if we can have 'narrative theory' should we not have 'thing theory'. In other words, as Roger-Pol Droit might ask, 'is Thing Theory a thing?' That there is no good answer to the question is neither here nor there. One can theorise about anything, and our theories create lenses through which we view and learn to understand different worlds. Indeed, one of my aims here is to suggest some alternatives. Just as there is no view from nowhere (nor any from nowhen) so there is no naïve or untheoretical approach to the world (see *axonometric projection*, §7). That said, choosing between different theoretical positions, for example, becomes a matter of personal choice and personal style (predilection perhaps). Anthropologists and other researchers must choose whether to place greater emphasis on theory or on ethnography. Of course, the best do both, presenting ethnography and theoretical development in interesting, exciting creative tension. But some pursue free-floating theory, safe from engagements with others (not in the academy); I take such engagement as an essential and valuable part of the ethnographic process.

The question originally posed by Roger-Pol Droit was in his book title, 'How Are Things?' (2005). Brown used the idea of 'thing theory' to bring back haptics and the experience of living in worlds full of recalcitrant things, each with its own quiddity. Even if on some accounts things can talk back, too often they seem not to attend to what we want of them. Attending and talking back may be part of Bruno Latour's widening of agency to include not only humans but also things and objects, such as automatic door closers. With agency comes the possibility of changing decisions, hence the work on the 'social life of things', including their cultural biographies. Leaving aside the delicate argument about the important differences between things and objects, we have to consider that every human society is a material one, composed of humans and a multiplicity of objects. Humans are imbricated with things, just as people are inseparable from their ecological environments. As João Pina-Cabral points out, building on Marilyn Strathern's work on gender and gift exchange, 'if we take to heart Mauss's discovery that the thing given is personified, then we must realize that persons are also aspects of things' (2020: 791).

Qv: *axonometric projection*

References

Brown, B. 2001. 'Thing Theory', *Critical Inquiry* 28: 1–22.

Droit, R.-P., and T. Cuffe. 2005. *How Are Things?: A Philosophical Experiment*. London: Faber.

Kopytoff, I. 1986. 'The Cultural Biography of Things: Commoditization as Process', in A. Appadurai (ed.), *The Social Life of Things: Commodities in Cultural Perspective*. Cambridge: Cambridge University Press, pp. 64–94.

Latour (Jim Johnson), B. 1988. 'Mixing Humans and Nonhumans Together: The Sociology of a Door-Closer', *Social problems* 35: 298–310.

Pina-Cabral, J. 2020. 'On Embracing the Vague', *HAU: Journal of Ethnographic Theory* 10: 786–99. https://doi.org/10.1086/711693.

Traces: see *Sgraffiti*

57. Translation (Anthropological Translation)

Geoffrey Lloyd pointed out that no anthropologist ever returned from the field announcing that they understood nothing from their fieldwork (2014: 222). The extreme cases of so-called untranslatability, where a term or concept is glossed as untranslatable, are misnamed. There are no terms that cannot be explained. Untranslatability means only that there is no simple, direct equivalence between target and source languages. This is a problem for literary translators but not for anthropologists. The extended discussions about Nuer concepts of twinship convey something of the connections seen by Nuer between twins and birds, so readers can gain a sense of their conceptual space. This does not help writers in other languages to write succinctly about those concepts, but that is not the point (Povinelli (2001) makes a similar argument). In an anthropological translation, a whole book may be needed to explain the range of meanings and nuances that a single word can evoke in a particular cultural setting (See Just and Zeitlyn 2014 Chapter 8).

It is by being *open*, rather than transparent, that anthropological translations can provide good evidence upon which to base arguments. Transparency implies invisibility, so they may not be noticed. Open translations may jar, but that makes the reader aware of them. An anthropological account is not only an ethnography but also a peg on which further ethnography can be hung (Bilmes 1996: 185 fn. 10). Hence, in preparing translations as anthropologists, our aim has been not to produce 'transparent' texts that could have been produced by native English speakers, but rather to produce intelligible texts that are anthropologically perspicuous. Werner distinguishes between 'front stage' and 'background' translations. The latter include 'extensive, encyclopaedic translator's notes' (1994: 61) including the ethnography, which is our main goal. They are intended to help readers unfamiliar with the society in question to understand some of the concepts under discussion, and to make available some of the evidence upon which the anthropologist's conclusions are based (Hermans (2002) and Povinelli (2001) reach similar conclusions, albeit in different ways). Viveiros de Castro expresses a similar ambition with the term *controlled equivocation* (§23).

So, in several different senses, one can view human society as being based on translation, and the process of translation as one in which meaning is negotiated between bilinguals. From this, it follows that there must be ways of studying the process, since negotiation is intersubjective: it is a public phenomenon, not locked inaccessibly in the heads of the individuals concerned. In such public translation events, exemplary instances can be used as pivots, or *boundary objects* (§10), around which discussions of translation hinge.

Qv: *boundary objects*; *equivocation*; *exemplar*

References

Bilmes, J. 1996. 'Problems and Resources in Analyzing Northern Thai Conversation for English Language Readers', *Journal of Pragmatics* 26: 171–88.

Hermans, T. 2002. 'Paradoxes and Aporias in Translation and Translation Studies', in A. Riccardi (ed.), *Translation Studies: Perspectives on an Emerging Discipline*. Cambridge: Cambridge University Press, pp. 1–23.

Just, R., and D. Zeitlyn. 2014. *Excursions in Realist Anthropology: A Merological Approach*. Newcastle upon Tyne: Cambridge Scholars Publishing.

Lloyd, G.E.R. 2014. 'On the Very Possibility of Mutual Intelligibility', *HAU: Journal of Ethnographic Theory* 4: 221–35.

Povinelli, E.A. 2001. 'Radical Worlds: The Anthropology of Incommensurability and Inconceivability', *Annual Review of Anthropology* 30: 319–34.

Werner, O. 1994. 'Ethnographic Translation: Issues and Challenges', *Sartoniana* 7: 59–135.

Travelling Concepts: see *Essentially Contested Concepts*

Triangulation: see *Teleoanalysis*

Uncertainty: see *Vagueness*

Underdetermination: see *Vagueness*

V

Vagueness; Vignettes

58. Vagueness

The entry on *partiality* (§45) argues for acceptance of incompleteness: our understanding and our accounts of that understanding may never be perfect; there is always new material that can reveal a fact not previously recognised. Discussions of vagueness complement those about partiality. The key here is to be clear about whether an account is itself vague (vague in its own terms, due to poor understanding) or whether it accurately conveys the external, real-world vagueness it describes. Recent work argues that there is perhaps less vagueness out there than is often assumed (although Pina-Cabral would disagree). Nonetheless, vagueness is an inevitable aspect of the world we live in and strive to understand. Describing it clearly is important because it is an indicator of the types of entanglement that occur in the fuzzy edges that simultaneously separate and link the issues with which we are concerned: people, things and concepts.

João Pina-Cabral outlines two 'doors of entanglement': the door of indeterminacy and the door of underdetermination. He argues that vagueness is 'out there', where there is less certainty (solidity perhaps) than we have conventionally believed. He concludes: 'The world of humans is foundationally vague both in that it is indeterminate and in that it is underdetermined; and it remains so to the end' (2020: 796). His argument shows the importance of actively considering vagueness in both our research practice (how we approach people and the social worlds they make) and our accounts of it. Those accounts should acknowledge both uncertainty and incompleteness (Pina-Cabral's doors) and perhaps also add a third mirrored door to reflect our own vagueness.

Mary Douglas discussed these issues in terms of indeterminacy. She said:

> The splendid thing about indeterminacy for anthropology is that our arcane problems about other people's thought suddenly become common to us all as human beings. We are all creatures that live in uncertainty, and have done from earliest times; while we cope with uncertainty as best we can, we go on seeking certainty. We create institutions that protect our valued ideas. We use analogies to build them up like a house of cards, one weak and fragile idea balanced against another, with a few central ideas holding them in place like a roof. (2001: 148)

Parallel to this position on vagueness is a similar argument about uncertainty. In effect, this involves asking whether uncertainty is ontological or epistemological. Is uncertainty an inevitable part of the world we live in, or can it be removed by more research? Could we turn uncertainty into certainty by learning more, by undertaking more research? Or would such endeavours just reveal more of the uncertainty out there? Trying to be clear about different types of vagueness can produce answers. Sometimes we should accept that we have reached real limits, and sometimes more work can reduce the vagueness.

Qv: *finitism*; *partiality*

References

Douglas, M. 2001. 'Dealing with Uncertainty', *Ethical Perspectives* 8: 145–55.
Pina-Cabral, J. 2020. 'On Embracing the Vague', *HAU: Journal of Ethnographic Theory* 10: 786–99.

59. Vignettes

An ethnographic vignette is a small case study typically from field research, an *exemplar* (§26) that illustrates and makes a wider point. Vignettes commonly focus on an epiphanic moment in a life story: a key turning point in the life of an individual, or sometimes of a community. The extended case study method, developed by the Manchester school of anthropology, uses vignettes in writing. Having material for a vignette does not mean it is the only such story available, although what is published may be the clearest example of the type and the best documented instance. Vignettes are the hooks from which hang ethnographic analysis, and hence wider sociological meaning. The analysis seeks to explain what participants are taking for granted, and how participants and onlookers understand what is going on. As one-off cases, vignettes can be described as fitting the 'method of specimens' developed by Philip Runkel (1990). In short, you need only find one live coelacanth to know that they are not extinct, known only as a fossil. Runkel contrasts this with what he calls 'the method of nets', a form of sampling in which the catch depends on the size of the net's mesh.

Parallel to vignettes are gobbets. These are short extracts of text, used in exams and in academic publishing. They are used as exemplars of a particular author's style and type of argument. Published work sometimes provides an argument made up of gobbets: a sequence of extended quotes from different authors, a particular danger with review articles. Contrastingly, ethnographic case studies are *mosaic* fragments (§40) from fieldwork that provide exemplars for anthropology. Another way of seeing it is that ethnographic gobbets are vignettes, *exemplars* (§26) of the ethnographic process. However, unlike exemplars, vignettes may be of unusual or aberrant cases: by explaining the origins of outliers, a vignette can be used to illuminate the commoner cases.

Individual vignettes resemble strands of a *cable* (§11) in that their strength depends not on each individual element but on the ensemble. They are of central importance to ethnography, the building blocks from which an ethnographic argument is constructed. As such, vignettes may be seen as having the importance of *epiphany* (§20) in *life writing* (§39). In life writing or ethnography, the epiphanic moments or vignettes have a wider significance (for both the subject and the anthropologist) than can be captured by blanket description.

To concentrate on a particular vignette or gobbet has entailments (which include *commitments* §16). To focus on one vignette, one case study, entails acceptance of the loss of focus on other aspects (without implying that one is true and others false). All we have are facets or glimpses, which ethnography does so well: the telling fieldwork example, the key case study. But we misunderstand these if we see them as teaching a single deep lesson. They teach us many lessons, which may be mutually contradictory. That returns us to *incommensurability* (§33) and the possibility of withholding (forbearing) from the making of judgments between alternatives.

Qv: cables; epiphanies; exemplars; hapax; isolarion; mosaics; non-ergodicity

Reference

Runkel, P.J. 1990. *Casting Nets and Testing Specimens: Two Grand Methods of Psychology*. New York: Praeger Publishers.

W

Wicked Problems

60. Wicked Problems

Wicked problems (Rittel and Webber 1973) are the decision-making version of *essentially contested concepts* (§24). Since one of these ideas comes from engineering and the other from political philosophy, it is not surprising that wicked problems were developed independently of their precursor. However, the basic parallel holds. The definitional paradigm case of a wicked problem is airport expansion. Consider Heathrow Airport to the west of London, where engineering crosses politics, crosses environmental concerns, crosses business pressures. The interested parties cannot all be satisfied by any one outcome. Steve Rayner saw wicked problems as resulting from 'contradictory certainties'.

'Wicked' problems are often those where the dynamic and behavioural complexities are high; where different groups of key decision makers hold different assumptions, values and beliefs, and where component problems cannot be solved in isolation from one another. Conversely, 'tame' problems (Rittel and Webber 1973) have low dynamic and behavioural complexity and can be solved using conventional analytical methods involving data collection and 'static' analysis (i.e. analysis that does not require dealing with delays, multiple feedback loops and non-linear relationships). Tame problems can be solved in isolation, can be broken down into parts that can be solved independently by different groups of people. Solutions to different parts of a larger problem can then be integrated into an overall solution. There is an old Japanese saying, 'If all you have is a hammer, then everything looks like a nail', and trying to solve 'wicked' problems using 'tame' problem-solving techniques will cause the wrong problem to be solved. (Lane and Woodman 2000)

The challenge for an academic studying wicked problems is to give a nuanced account that can describe and explain the 'paths of wickedness' (and probably the absence of any possible 'paths of righteousness' in the form of solutions agreeable to all parties). It may be impossible to be *faithful* (§27) to all the parties, and some form of *ironic detachment* (§36) is inevitable. As noted in the entry on *essentially contested concepts* (§24), an important deflationary tactic is to choose our terms of analysis very carefully so as to avoid building in or importing the wicked problem in the way we give our accounts. As analysts, we should employ plain and uncontentious language, and I emphasise again language that is knowingly incomplete.

Qv: *boundary objects*; *essentially contested concepts*

References

Lane, R., and G. Woodman. 2000. 'Wicked Problems, Righteous Solutions: Back to the Future on Large Complex Projects', Proceedings 8th Annual Meeting of the International Group for Lean Construction, 17–19 August 2000, Brighton, UK.

Rittel, H.W., and M.M. Webber. 1973. 'Dilemmas in a General Theory of Planning', *Policy sciences* 4: 155–69.

Withholding: see *Forbearing*

Coda

So What?

A Worked Example of Making Sense of Ethnographic Fragments

The more I know what really happened, the more I wonder if there is a 'what really happened'
　　　—I. Hacking, 'Two Souls in One Body'

How can this type of approach work in actual ethnographic analysis?[1] While no single case study is likely to apply all the concepts listed in this book, theoretical flexibility can enhance both understanding and explication. I present a small piece of ethnography as a worked example of tessellated ethnography: in other words, of treating ethnographic analysis as an exercise in mosaic making as much as narrative storytelling. There always is storytelling. But the contextualisation and explanations to make sense of the narrative should have the shimmer of mosaic. And like all mosaic, the gaps should show.

An Ethnographic Snippet: Arguing during *Ngwun*

Presenting ethnography to the uninitiated is not straightforward. Little can be taken for granted, so various explanations must be given to cater for a wide and varied readership. Some Mambila and other expert readers may regard this as stating the obvious, as dangerously oversimplifying or overemphasising problems behind the scenes, rather than concentrating on the final performance that most people experience. I look forward to discussions about how to summarise an event in ways that are simultaneously sympathetic to local sensitivities and comprehensible to strangers.

An Introduction to Mambila

The Mambila people live on either side of the Nigeria-Cameroon border, mostly on the Mambila Plateau in Nigeria.[2] A smaller number (around 12,000) live in Cameroon, especially at the foot of the Mambila Plateau escarpment, on the Tikar Plain. My fieldwork has concentrated on these groups, and particularly on the village of Somié. According to the official (if contentious) 1986 tax census, Somié then had a population of approximately one thousand. The village centre now has over five thousand residents, as a combined result of endogenous population growth and immigration of Mambila from Nigeria. Self-sufficient in food, some villagers have grown coffee as a cash crop since the early 1960s, although this is of diminishing economic importance; by 2010 palm oil and maize were also being farmed as cash crops.

Cameroonian Mambila on the Tikar Plain have a social structure that closely resembles that described among the Nigerian villagers of Warwar by Rehfisch (1972) based on his fieldwork in 1953. According to his reports, Nigerian Mambila had no institutionalised chiefship resembling that of the Cameroonian Mambila villages. In Nigeria, villages were organised on gerontocratic principles and largely lacked political offices. In Cameroon, they adopted the Tikar institution of the chiefship, with few changes. Rehfisch's fieldnotes[3] make clear that in Warwar there was a sort of chief: in charge of ritual but without political influence. I believe that this formed the kernel of the institution now existing in Cameroonian Mambila villages. The ritual chief provided a Mambila armature onto which the Tikar style of chiefship could be attached. Other models of power in Cameroon come from the city-state of Foumban and the Grassfield polities to the south, and the Lamidate[4] of Banyo to the North, which ruled over most of the Tikar Plain.

The chiefship was bolstered by the effects of French colonial administration. This rubber-stamped the appointment of chiefs from the very first inspection tours in the early 1920s. It is uncertain whether the Chief then had as much authority as now, and I have tried unsuccessfully to find data to clarify the issue. However, it is revealing that one old man in Somié, discussing the genealogy of its chiefs, denied that Tulum (who came from Mvɔr in Nigeria[5]), the founding ancestor of the chiefs of Somié, Sonkolong and Atta villages, was himself a chief.

The institution of chiefship is now well established, and since independence in 1960 the national government has continued the colonial policy of underwriting chiefs' authority, a policy that makes traditional rulers into agents of the state.[6] A village chief in contemporary Cameroon has a dual role. Within the village, he exercises executive authority; for example, organising communal labour (most importantly: maintaining the road). In his judicial capacity, he hears disputes brought to his palace, acting as arbitrator in the first instance and as chairman in tribunal hearings before the village Notables. He also represents the village before the external authorities, including the administrative officers and the gendarmerie. Reciprocally, he acts as their mouthpiece in the village, reporting news from the local administrative centre (Bankim) and decisions affecting the village.

In summary, Mambila are a relatively small ethnic group living in the Nigerian and Cameroonian borderlands in the broad middle area where ecological and cultural norths meet their respective souths. Never centralised as a group, the Mambila in Cameroon have adopted some institutions from the Tikar people to their east (although this claim is not as straightforward as it may seem) and have had chiefs who exercise power with the sanction of the national state.

Royal Ritual: The *Ngwun* Rite

Many groups in this part of Cameroon (southwards of Somié) have royal rituals with cognate names. Perhaps the most celebrated is the *Nguoun* festival (as it is now called), celebrated in the large city-state of Foumban, some 250 km south of Somié. There is clearly a general model of royal ritual widely distributed over a long period;[7] I next describe very briefly the Mambila variant as practised in Somié.

In essence, the *Ngwun* rite is a biennial re-enactment of the chief's installation, during which he repeats his 'oath of office'. The rite involves both private and public elements. The public ritual is a theatrical performance in which representatives from outlying hamlets, who owe allegiance to the chief, enact their subservience in a war dance around the chief's palace. In this dance, people from the village fight those from the outlying hamlets; the former are beaten back, but the warriors from the hamlets acquiesce when confronted by the person of the chief. In the private ritual, the Chief is treated with special medicines to prevent evil actions (conceptualised as witchcraft) whether by others or himself. The treatments also promote his fertility, and by extension that of the village. Most of the private rites are performed in the innermost house of the palace by the ritual specialists, *mgbe lə* (lit. the chiefs of the medicine), who also have overall control of the entire performance. In 1994, I was permitted to witness these private rites, of which I had never previously been able even to elicit a description. I have subsequently participated in several *Ngwun* performances as an untitled *mgbe lə* (see Figures 2 and 3), including in the processions from inside the palace out into the public dance (Figure 4).

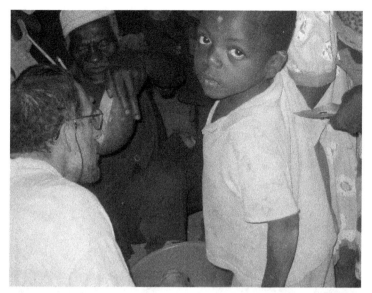

Figure 2. David Zeitlyn being treated inside the palace during *Ngwun* in December 2004. © David Zeitlyn.

Figure 3. *Mgbe lə* ritual leaders and DZ ready for the *Ngwun* procession in 2000. © David Zeitlyn.

Figure 4. The *Ngwun* procession leaving the palace in 2000. The chief wears a large hat and follows the *mgbe lə*. © David Zeitlyn.

Before leaving the palace, the chief repeats his oath of office. Only his wives, senior titled women (the *Marenjo*[8]) and the *mgbe lə* may attend the oath-taking in the innermost enclosure of the palace, but selected seniors are allowed to listen to his words from within the palace but outside the innermost fence.

Once the main ritual treatment has been performed in private, the chief, the *mgbe lə*, the *Marenjo* and the chief's wives process out of the royal palace into the public square. They circle the square, surrounded by dancers, while the crowd bows. The chief and his senior sister then sit on royal stools and drink three gourds of beer while the onlookers cheer. Some senior participants (a *mgbe lə* and a daughter of one of the chief's sisters) tour the village blessing every house to protect the occupants from evil and to promote their fertility.

In sum, this complex ritual has different components, each with many participants. There is no single 'correct' account of *Ngwun*, even from a single Mambila village: different participants have very different understandings of the event.

In the thirty days before the main dance, various preliminary rituals are held. At the start of this period, the chief is blessed by the ritual specialists before being ceremonially led into his house, where he remains in seclusion. Some rituals are performed privately inside the chief's palace before the actors move outside to involve the whole village. The preliminary rituals also include treating each house and its occupants. The chief is supposed to eat richly during this period and is painted red with camwood and oil so that when he eventually appears in public he is plump and glistening: the exemplification of health. He personifies the health of the body politic, the whole village, evoking Frazer's discussion of divine kingship.

Seniority and Who Knows What?

The 2004–2005 performance of *Ngwun* had particular significance for two of the participants. For Chief Ndi Adam, this was the first performance of *Ngwun* since his installation as chief. For Gangfi Daniel, it was the first *Ngwun* for which he was the most senior ritual leader, and hence 'in charge'. The implications of both of these statements require explanation. A new Chief comes unknowing to the rituals because of the secrecy surrounding the innermost, hidden ritual. The concern is less with secrecy from the general public than with secrecy from the 'princes': the royal males eligible for selection as chief. The principal fear (of the ritual chiefs and those in the Palace) is that some of these candidates for succession might become impatient and make a claim for the throne. For this reason, they are excluded from the rituals that support and enhance the authority of the current chief. The strict prohibitions repeatedly stressed by ritual chiefs against revealing details of the rites to other members of the royal family have constrained what I have felt able to publish about *Ngwun*.[9]

Seniority among the ritual leaders and among the *Marenjo*, although age-related, is not strictly gerontocratic: it does *not* derive solely from the age of the title holders. For a long time I thought that the titles were ranked by age. In a way they are, but not in the sense that a ranked list remains current over the years. Seniority derives from longevity in post. Akin to a tontine (a savings group in which the last survivor inherits all the assets), the most senior person in the group is its longest-serving member. Seniority follows time in post whichever title is held: strictly, age is irrelevant. In practice, the longest-serving member is usually the oldest, but this is not always the case: a young person could be selected for one title before an older person is given another. Over time, the younger of the two will become the longer-serving title holder, so they and their title will be regarded as the most senior. This system sometimes results in issues about the relative authority of the various seniors. In 2004–2005, Gangfi had become the most senior and was therefore 'in charge' of the ritual for *Ngwun*. However, he was not on good terms with the second most senior ritual leader, who was a few years his elder. Another factor that hampers the organisation of the ritual is that most people's memories of previous performances are more or less impaired by the effects of alcohol. So discussions often become heated. In the end, though, it doesn't matter: everyone in the village agrees that what is important is that the ritual takes place, and if afterwards it is realised that a detail has been omitted (as sometimes happens), then a mental note is taken so that next time *Ngwun* is done better.[10]

The Run-up to *Ngwun* 2004–2005

On 18 December 2004, one of the preliminary rites to *Ngwun* was performed. The ritual leaders were administering initial blessings to the Chief and those around him before ceremo-

Figure 5. Photo from 2004: *Mgbe lə* Wela treating *Marenjo* Korobon. Another ritual leader, Joseph Ndibi, stands behind. © David Zeitlyn.

nially leading him into seclusion in his palace. But there are things the ritual leaders cannot do alone: some parts of the ritual require the presence of at least one *Marenjo*. After the Chief and his first wife had been blessed and led indoors, the blessing of the children could not begin until one *Marenjo* was present. Here everything stalled.

While waiting, all those present drank palm wine (and in some cases sachets of commercially processed spirits), so by the time the most senior *Marenjo* arrived, an element of disorder had begun to emerge. Nonetheless, the blessings of the children began, and all went smoothly until another *Marenjo* arrived, full of indignation that she had been delayed. Figure 4 shows one of the *Marenjo* being treated before she herself started treating the children.

At the time, I did not understand what was going on, and I am still uncertain about much of it. However, on the following day, I recorded a discussion with the *Marenjo* in question about what had happened, and my reconstruction of events is based on that conversation helped by entries in diaries being kept for me by several people in the village. (The diaries and their writers are discussed in Zeitlyn 2010.)

Competing to be Chief-Maker: Choosing *Marenjo*s and *Papa*s

Papa is the title of the head of Gumbe hamlet, one of two chief-makers responsible for choosing the new Chief of Somié. The population of Gumbe is held to descend from a sister of the first chief of Somié.[11] Descent through the female line disqualifies anyone from Gumbe from succeeding to the chiefship. Having kinship ties, and lacking the power to depose him, they are trusted allies of the chief.[12]

Some years previously, Yokoten, a son of *Papa* Njaibi, had hoped to become head of Gumbe but had not been chosen. Diary entries written in those preceding years reveal some of the history to, and consequences of, his not being chosen (the failure to succeed to power). In one case (on 9 March 1999), he had caused offence at the hearing of a dispute by seeming to adopt the role of senior arbitrator, despite the presence, in good health, of *Papa* Ŋenedɔŋ, his full brother. The diary entry recording the argument makes it clear that this hubris was seen as more important than the original field dispute. Yokoten had been passed over for the headship when his father died in March 1994. Before this, there had been a public quarrel (also recorded in diary entries) between Yokoten and his father (Njaibi), who said he should never become *Papa*.[13] There were also rumours that Yokoten was implicated in Njaibi's death (according to some, by overdosing him with quinine). This was cited by some informants as the cause of a fight between Yokoten and his younger brother, Ŋenengwe. Following this fight, Yokoten left Gumbe to live in another hamlet on the far side of Somié. He told me that this move was due to the illness of his children (implicitly caused by witchcraft). However, other people from both Gumbe and Somié described his move as an exile. Several years later, after mediation and the performance of ritual oaths in which he swore his innocence, Yokoten moved back to Gumbe. Then, when the next *Papa* (Ŋenedɔŋ) died in December 2003, fresh rumours circulated that he was responsible for this death. Such is the currency of local political infighting. This explains why an apparently trivial event (publicly shouting at someone, when Yokoten and his father Njaibi had quarrelled, as mentioned above) was taken so seriously: that is how a pretender would act.

Other diary entries[14] refer indirectly to continuing disputes between Yokoten and his brother, Ŋenedɔŋ, after the latter became *Papa*. These contemporaneous records enable us to track the political campaign over the years more reliably than any later reconstruction of events, when accounts would inevitably be 'edited' by people's memories and in the light of intervening events. Since all retrospective accounts are affected by the outcomes of the events they describe, contemporary diary records are particularly valuable in avoiding corrections of hindsight. When villagers talked of *Papa* Ŋenedɔŋ in 2004, it was in the light of his sudden death in December 2003. Whether or not Yokoten was implicated in that death, he survived, and his brother did not. Many people felt there was only one possible conclusion: that witchcraft was involved in Ŋenedɔŋ's sudden illness and death (see Fisiy and Geschiere 1996 and Geschiere 1997 for parallel cases from elsewhere in Cameroon).

By December 2004, no successor to *Papa*[15] was in place. I was told that Yokoten had been selected in principle but that he was too ill to be installed (he was then recovering from surgery in hospital, 200 km away in Foumban). Having been told by several people that he had been selected, I and many residents of Somié were surprised when on 2 January 2005 Mvulu Jonas (a cousin of Yokoten) was formally made *Papa*, in time to participate in the *Ngwun* ritual scheduled for 10 January 2005. The decision was apparently made at a meeting of people from Gumbe with the chief of Somié after a small group of seniors had failed to come to a decision. (It was emphasised to me that divination was *not* performed to assist this decision-making process, divination being reserved for the choice of the chief). Following this meeting, the ritual leaders (the *mgbe lə*, who organise the *Ngwun* rite) were told whom to install as Papa. The decision-makers were prepared to say about their decision only that Yokoten was not well enough to return in time to participate in *Ngwun*. People in the village, hearing this result, inferred that his state of health swayed the decision. Indeed, some of my discussants took the outcome to imply that the decision-makers saw his state of health as a verdict of complicity in the preceding deaths. It may be fairer to see it, as another of my Mambila friends put it, as fate (*sàgà*[16]): on this account, had he recovered in time to return to the village, he would have been chosen.[17] By not returning, he missed his chance. So history is made.

But why was the *Marenjo* so late, and why so cross? Writing about this long after the event, I am keenly aware of all the questions I did not ask and all the things I was not told. What follows is informed speculation. When I talked to her the next day, she said she was cross because they, the sons of Njaibi, were 'cooking people in a pot and eating them' (the classic actions of witches; the eating is said to take place mystically, from the inside). I prompted with names, and she said that Yokoten had eaten Ŋenedɔŋ. I accepted her explanation on her terms. Confronted with the enormity of her anger, it seemed impossible then to ask why she had been late for the ritual; so I never found out specifically what delayed her arrival at the palace.

In December 2004, Somié's ritual and political organisation was disturbed because there was not only no *Papa* but also no *Marenjo* from Gumbe. The selection of *Marenjo* is informal, made by the existing *Marenjo* in consultation with elder women from the place in question (for the *Marenjo*, from Njere and Gumbe) and then reported to the chief. (This is very similar to the process of choosing the next *Papa*, although in that case the chief of Somié plays a role in the decision-making.) Given the day's events and her comments on the following day, my inference is that the *Marenjo* in question had been in Gumbe to discuss the choice of the new Gumbe *Marenjo* and while there had become involved in an argument about who had killed Ŋenedɔŋ through witchcraft and hence in the dispute about who was to become the next *Papa*. Finally, it is worth noting that the woman selected as *Marenjo* for Gumbe (installed just before *Ŋgwun* on 8 January 2005) was Dada Ndenɔŋ, a daughter of Yokoten. As a consequence, the families of the rival cousins in Gumbe have to continue working together on formal occasions such as *Ŋgwun*. The families of the cousins Yokoten and Mvulu have to work together and be seen to work together through the roles held by Mvulu and Ndenɔŋ. For all the rivalry between the families, these roles constitute formal social ties that may help counteract private suspicions and competition. This is my summary using my analytic vocabulary. Mambila actors talk of cooling livers (hearts) and smoothing out problems. Both are ways of comprehending and describing how wider factors impinge on the micropolitics of individuals as they live their lives.

Coda: Back to Theory

As I have said, one worked example can never illustrate or use all the theoretical approaches that are sketched in the main part of this book. Readers may find connections with other parts, but I would connect this account particularly with the following sections: first and foremost *partiality* and *incompleteness*. This case study is also closely connected to the discussion of *exemplars* and *vignettes*. Issues of *translation* of course are pervasive: Did I understand the Mambila conversations? More generally, did I understand the events taking place? Is my account fair to what was said and what happened (partly through those words being said)? This links the topics of *translation* and *faithfulness*. Ultimately, my account is knowingly incomplete: I have tried to present a sort of *mosaic* that conveys some of the complexity of how interacting and overlapping aspects of human life produce effects, some of them predictable and desirable but many of them unintended. The ethnographic account provides a starting point for apprehending and appreciating the textures of this richly dappled world.

Notes

1. With thanks to Michael Herzfeld, who challenged me, in effect, to put up or shut up.
2. More detail is in Zeitlyn 1994.
3. These are available as part of the Experience Rich Anthropology project at http://era.anthropology.org.uk/Era_Resources/Era/Rehfisch/.
4. An Islamic kingdom owing suzerainty to the Sultan of Ngaoundéré.
5. The village of Mvɔr, now abandoned, is at the top of the Mambila Plateau escarpment (very close to the international border). The site was documented by Jean Hurault (1986, 1988).

6. The chief of Somié, as a state-recognised 'chief, third class', is entitled to a monthly salary from the state.

7. This is not the place to discuss the implications of that shared history. I am working on a monograph about the ritual and its organisation.

8. Each of the women known as the *Marenjo* (a Fulfulde term: the Mambila term *gə mgbe* is now archaic) has a distinct title. They are often referred to collectively in French as the 'princesses', although not all are kin of the chief, some being the chosen representatives of outlying hamlets, such as Gumbe.

9. This is the reason why I have not written the '*Ngwun* for Dummies' manual that Chief Ndi suggested I should have written!

10. This is what Roy Wagner calls 'inventive improvisation' (1981: 66).

11. Other informants believe descent to be through a brother, although that account does not explain their lack of eligibility for chiefship.

12. The other chief-maker is the head of the Njerup, a Mambila group, who having invited the chief's people to assist them in a local war are thereby held to have ceded any right to the chiefship.

13. In effect, this disinherited him from being selected as *Papa*; although officially the incumbent does not choose his successor, this statement will have been taken into account by the group of elders who selected the next *Papa*.

14. The diarist who recorded the argument in March 1999 mentioned Yokoten again on 9 May 1999; another diarist wrote about him on 23 December 2000.

15. I am talking here about offices including the title and role of the Gumbe headship. It must be admitted that the hamlet is not large, and the office is not onerous.

16. This is not to be taken in a fully deterministic sense: an alternative translation would be 'chance'. The Mambila term sums up his bad luck and the sense of the fixity of the past, without necessarily evoking its preordination. (*Sàgà* is a Fulfulde loan word.) Mambila ideas of fate are discussed in more detail in Zeitlyn 2020.

17. This was local speculation: the person who said this was not one of the decision-makers.

References

Fisiy, C., and P. Geschiere 1996. 'Witchcraft, Violence and Identity: Different Trajectories in Postcolonial Cameroon', in R.P. Werbner and T.O. Ranger (eds), *Post-Colonial Identities in Africa*. London: Zed books, pp. 193–222.

Geschiere, P. 1997. *The Modernity of Witchcraft: Politics and the Occult in Post-colonial Africa*. London: University of Virginia Press.

Hacking, I. 1991. 'Two Souls in One Body', *Critical Inquiry* 17: 838–67.

Hurault, J.M. 1986. 'Les Anciens Peuplements de Cultivateurs de L'Adamaoua Occidental (Cameroun-Nigeria)', *Cah. Sci. Hum.* 22: 115–45.

———. 1988. 'A Report on Archaeological Surveys in the Cameroon-Nigeria Border Region', *Africa* 58: 470–76.

Rehfisch, F. 1972. *The Social Structure of a Mambila Village* (Occ. Paper 2). Zaria: Ahmadu Bello University: Sociology Department.

Wagner, R. 1981. *The Invention of Culture*. Chicago: University of Chicago Press.

Zeitlyn, D. 1994. *Sua in Somié: Mambila Traditional Religion*. Sankt Augustin: Academia Verlag.

———. 2010. 'Diary Evidence for Political Competition: Mambila Autoethnography and Pretensions to Power', *African Studies Review* 53(2): 77–95.

———. 2020. *Mambila Divination: Framing Questions, Constructing Answers*. London: Routledge.

Index